Calling All Miriams

Ordinary Women, Extraordinary Ministries

Sue Towne

Scrolls of Zebulon
A Publishing Company
Scrolls of Zebulon LLC
Mobile, Alabama US

Calling All Miriams

For more information, visit www.CallingAllMiriams.com

Scrolls of Zebulon, LLC
P.O. Box 190309
Mobile, Alabama, USA
ScrollsOfZebulon.com
For inquiries, contact info@scrollsofzebulon.com

Cover Design by Sharon Taylor
Interior Design by Sarah Smith
Chapter Art by Susan C. Towne
Edited by Layne Prince

All scripture quotations are from the New American Standard translation unless otherwise noted.

ISBN: 979-8-9880223-0-5

LCCN: 2023905586

For Worldwide Distribution

Printed in the USA

Table of Contents

V

VI

To the One who
calls me "Miriam"...

INTRODUCTION TO THE NAME "MIRIAM"

One day as I was listening to a man prophesying to a group of women, likening them to Miriam the sister of Moses, I realized that God was saying, "Calling all Miriams!" just as loudly as He could. What did He mean, "Calling all Miriams"?

I found the beginnings of an answer to my question by taking a look at the amazing **Miriams** of Scripture. And I know that the Bible-literate among you are thinking, "Miriams? I can think of only one Miriam in the Bible."

Well actually, I am going to fashion some brief word portraits of **seven** Miriams mentioned in the Bible.

Each Miriam is an example of one or more types of ministry that God calls us to, whether we are male or female. I believe that God wants us to see that there is no male or female in Christ—that is, no gender barriers in the spirit realm as to the ministry we can have in the Kingdom of Heaven, even here on the earth. As Paul observed in Galatians 3:28, ***"There is neither Jew nor Greek, there is neither slave nor free, there is neither male nor female; for you are all one in Christ Jesus."***

The idea that God does not use women in ministry, especially in high-visibility leadership positions in the Church, has been passé for decades now, at least in many parts of the Body of Christ on the earth. Yet I find many women who still do not believe that they have as important a role in God's Kingdom on earth as they see men have.

Today we're going to take away the excuse, "Oh, I could never do *that*—I'm a *woman*!" For some we will also be cutting through stereotypes about what God thinks about who qualifies to minister in the Kingdom. And while we're at it, let's stop thinking about God as someone far away and separated from our lives. Let's call him "Father," a name He likes to be called by His children.

And let's call Jesus by his Hebrew/Aramaic name, "Yeshua" (yeh-SHOO-ah). In my own personal experience with the Lord, I have found that my relationship with Him went to a far deeper level when I began to call Him "Yeshua," rather than "Jesus."

I grew up around Christianity, but I never had a deep or living relationship with God in my early years. My family attended a Protestant church, maybe once or twice a month. I was familiar with the Sunday-school version of Jesus. You know what I mean: the "poster Jesus" who was surrounded by children, who carried a lamb on his shoulders, who preached from a fishing boat, and was good at teaching the people about God. I was always puzzled as a child why this innocuous Jesus made the religious authorities so angry, why he got arrested, and why he was executed.

Fast forward in my life to the age of 30. I won't spend time on the details here, but a series of events in my life built to a decision point. At a time when I was faced with a set of life and-death issues importuning my heart, I literally surrendered to God by praying a sort of desperate prayer, accepting the salvation that Jesus died to give me. I had so little faith in what I was praying, that I ended my prayer that day by saying, *"And if there's nothing to any of this, I know that nothing will come of it."*

But something *did* come of that prayer. It turned the rudder of my life a hard 180 degrees. Whereas in the past I never gave the Bible a second thought, now I began to read it voraciously. I started attending a local church every Sunday, not because I "had to," but because I wanted to be with people who knew this Jesus, and I wanted to know Him better.

As I began to study the Scriptures, I found myself drawn more and more to also study the customs of Bible times, so that I could begin to understand why the people in Scripture said certain things and did certain things. Fairly early in this new phase of my life, I discovered the wonderful name, "**Yeshua**." Yes, it literally means, "the salvation of God." But in the richness of the Hebrew language and culture, it means so much more: well-being, deliverance, prosperity, victory. As I began to refer to Jesus as "Yeshua" and to address Him that way in my prayer, I found that new dimensions of knowing Him on a personal one-on-one level began to open up to me, and I am still experiencing new dimensions with Him every day.

But enough about me. Let's lay a foundation for what I want to share with you about the name "**Miriam**." What does that name mean?

Scholars have several interesting theories concerning the origin of that name. One theory is that Miriam comes from the Hebrew word *"maree"*[1] (ma-REE), meaning "*bitterness, rebellion, or strength.*" The root word in Hebrew for this word is *"marar"*[2] (ma-RAR), meaning "*to be or to make bitter or unpleasant, to rebel or to resist, to provoke, to be disobedient.*"

Okay. Strength is a positive attribute, but bitterness and rebellion? Who would hang a name on their daughter with *that* meaning, especially in an ancient culture, where names prophesied destiny?

1 Hebrew ירמ
2 Hebrew ררמ

Consequently I looked a little deeper. I found that some linguists related the name Miriam to the word "myrrh" (מור in Hebrew). Myrrh is an herbal substance distilled from the sap of the myrrh tree, which grows in the Middle East. Myrrh is bitter to the taste but has a very sweet fragrance. So maybe there is a bittersweet quality about women named Miriam.

That sounded a little better. Maybe despite the bitterness of life, they give off a sweet fragrance.

But I still could not picture one of those wall plaques you see in some gift stores with the name "Miriam" on it and the definition "*bittersweet*" printed beneath it. Digging deeper still, I discovered another linguistic theory linking Miriam to an ancient Egyptian word, "*marye*" (meh-RAY), which means "*beloved.*"

Beloved—that's more like the kind of thing I would want my name to mean if I were Miriam. But ironically, as I researched the lives of the Miriams in Scripture, I began to see that their lives reflected a combination of bitter and sweet, with a streak of rebellion and considerable strength. (Perhaps rebellion and strength are two sides of the same coin.) But above all, these Miriams were BELOVED—the beloved of the Father!

With that in mind, I'm going to present to you a series of mini-portraits—vignettes—from the life of each one of these Miriams. My hope is that you will discover some things about each one of these women that you never considered before. Each one of these women is an everyday, average woman of her culture—yet an absolutely extraordinary adventurous risk-taker, breaking even the religious stereotypes about women in our own day, let alone in her day!

This book can either be read by individuals or used for group study and discussion. At the beginning of each chapter, I have suggested Scripture reading that would be especially helpful for readers who are not very familiar with the stories I talk about in that chapter.

At the end of each chapter, I have posed several questions for readers to think about and then either journal the reader's particular answers or discuss those with a group.

The final chapter of this book has several suggested exercises designed to help readers expand their view of their own lives and help them discover possibilities they never thought of. Having said all that to prepare you, let's dive in....

I

THE MIRIAM WE THINK WE KNOW

Scripture Preview:
Exodus 1 to 2:1-8

The first Miriam mentioned in Scripture is the sister of Moses and Aaron, and we first meet her in Exodus chapter 2 as **"Miriam, the Watcher."**

This is a young girl, maybe nine or ten years old,[3] who is watching over her three-month-old brother, Moses, as he floats in the reeds of the Nile River. You recall that the Pharaoh had ordered the death of all newborn male Hebrew children. Even though he had enslaved the Hebrew population, Pharaoh feared their growing numbers. He reasoned, somewhat delusionally, that this minority population was a potential threat to his dynasty in the event of war. For that reason he told the Hebrew midwives to kill the newborn boy babies.

Of course, the Hebrew midwives did not want to carry out this horrific edict. Help a woman give birth to a perfectly healthy child and then kill it? You can't be serious. That's government-mandated infanticide.

3 Historians estimate that Miriam and her two brothers lived sometime between 1400 and 1300 BC.

At least two of the Hebrew midwives figured out a way around this. When they were summoned by the Egyptian officials to explain their lack of dead-baby body count, they said, "The Hebrew women are so vigorous that the babies are already born before we can get there."

They lied. They flat-out lied, and God apparently forgave them. Scripture says they were rewarded with families of their own because "they feared God" (Exodus 1:21). If we ever needed evidence about what God thinks of the killing of innocent babies, we have it here.

But back to our story. Why is baby Moses floating in the river? Well, after the midwives foiled the Pharaoh's plan, he issued another edict that every Hebrew boy born must be thrown into the Nile River. Kill the boys, but let all the Hebrew baby girls live. The irony is that the Pharaoh does not see the girls as any threat to him. But whether it's the midwives, the mother of Moses, his sister Miriam, or the daughter of Pharaoh, **the women in this story are consistently able to circumvent the arrogant will of this Pharaoh.**

Clearly, he underestimates the power of determined females. More importantly, he underestimates the power and wisdom of the holy God who protects the life of little Moses, the eventual deliverer of Israel. Isn't it so like the Lord to confound the wisdom of those who are wise in their own eyes by bringing the deliverance of the deliverer through the hands of those who were lowly and despised in that culture? This is God's frequent M.O.[4] He likes to use what looks like weakness to bring down the strong.

When little Moses was born to a woman named Jochebed[5] (JO-kah-bed), his mother saw that he was a beautiful baby boy and hid him for three months. Considering how noisy a baby

---

4 "M.O." is an abbreviation for the Latin phrase "modus operandi," meaning "typical way of doing things."

5 See Exodus 6:20, where her name is first mentioned.

can be, I'm wondering how she managed that. There must have been a conspiracy of silence with her neighbors. But at that three month mark, she realized she could not hide him any longer.

Therefore she complied with the Egyptian edict. She threw him in the river...in a wicker basket...covered with tar and pitch so that it would float and not sink. Wise woman. Scripture does not say whether she prayed, but I'm thinking she did pray, because of what happened next. And I also think Jochebed had a plan beyond just setting him adrift in the river, because the text says she *set* the little basket-boat among the reeds by the riverbank. Possibly, she knew that this was where the daughter of Pharaoh or some other wealthy woman was likely to come to bathe in the river.

Jochebed left. She may have set her daughter Miriam to watch over baby Moses. Or maybe little Miriam stayed because she had the curiosity of a kid. In any case, she stood at a distance to find out what would happen to her brother.

Ministry of the Watch

So what ministry was this young Miriam modeling for us? I would say that right here, right at this point in the story, she is a **watcher**. She is an example of our own call to watch over what goes on around us, sometimes for the purpose of taking action in the natural realm BUT other times to inform our prayers. Obvious examples of this involve our watching over family members. But we can also watch over friends, over coworkers, over neighbors, over famous people in trouble—or over complete strangers whom we encounter briefly in the streets of our community.

A simple example of this comes to mind. Do you ever read the bumper stickers of the car sitting ahead of you at the stoplight? I do. In my community some of their messages are a little hair-raising, spiritually speaking. But I use them as a springboard to pray for the persons driving that car, that the Father would draw them into the heart of His Son—that they would be freed from ungodly influences or even from the possible idol or demon worship implied by their bumper sticker!

For most of my life I have lived in a large, culturally diverse metropolitan area, where people of many faiths—and no faith at all—live. When I see folks dressed in garb identifying them as adherents of Islam or Judaism in particular, my heart is drawn to pray for them to be connected into the heart of the Son of God. They are complete strangers to me, yet my heart is drawn to pray for them, that they would have a life-changing encounter with Him.

Think about this: There are lots of simple, practical ways we watch over people as we go about life. What about the times someone near you drops money or a train ticket or a glove or a hat, and you swoop down to pick it up and restore it to them—sometimes running after the person to do so? What about the young mom with toddlers in tow who is also pushing a cart loaded with bags of groceries to her SUV? Hmmm, could it be that you are there by divine appointment to help her, even if it is just to return the empty cart for her?

Don't minimize these "little" things. The older I get, the more I appreciate it when a complete stranger helps me. This is ministry. Being watchful for these opportunities to be of help to others is part of the "watching" ministry. It's about putting my eyes on others, rather than being absorbed in my own problems or situations.

And to take all this a step further, we need to become watchers in the spirit, asking God what He wants prayed or declared and released into the lives of people. We need to ask what He wants us to do as individuals—instead of thinking we know what to pray or we know how to fix the situation. And then we release requests or declarations that are self-focused, self-indulgent, or just plain arrogant. I suspect that many times our well-intentioned but uninformed prayers get in the way of what our Father is trying to work out in someone's life.

Miriam the Quick-witted Intercessor

Notice that Miriam's ministry of "watching" leads her right into another ministry: the **ministry of intercession**. What is an intercessor? It's someone who speaks up on behalf of another. Often this intercession is directed to someone in a more powerful position than the person whom the intercessor is representing. It takes boldness and quick thinking sometimes to step up and speak up for someone who can't speak for themselves at that moment.

Here in Exodus 2, Miriam has the quick wit to step forward boldly and arrange with Pharaoh's daughter for Miriam's own mother Jochebed to be paid by Pharaoh's daughter to mother her own child, baby Moses! Do you realize how astonishing this is? Jochebed is a slave woman. She doesn't normally get paid to do anything! But now she is being paid to *nurse her own son*, the one that Pharaoh decreed should die! And at some point Moses will be brought into Pharaoh's palace to be educated in the culture and knowledge of Egypt, which was the greatest civilization of its day.

All because a little girl was watching and spoke up at the right time.

This is an example to us that intercession is not simply about prayers addressed to Heaven. It can also be about being a mediator for justice here on earth. By "justice" here I mean bringing things on earth into right alignment with Heaven's culture and values. In Heaven's culture baby boys and baby girls are cherished and valued—not killed. By her intercession that day, Miriam advanced Heaven's agenda on earth.

This kind of intercession in the natural realm probably

happens in your life more often than you think. Are you ever in conversation with a small group of people when one person in the group struggles to find the right word to express her situation? If you are familiar with her situation and can explain it clearly to the others in the group, you are helping to join together the two ends of this conversation for a right result.

Or like Miriam, do you overhear someone's dilemma and kindly step forward with a suggested solution? In that moment, you are acting as a go-between, between the dilemma and the solution. That's the very pattern of what we call intercession, isn't it?

Miriam the Prophet

Years later, we get another picture of this same Miriam, now advanced in years and experience with the Lord, as the Hebrew people are making their exodus from Egypt. Take a look:

> ***Miriam the prophetess,*** *Aaron's sister, took the timbrel in her hand, and all the women went out after her with timbrels and with dancing. Miriam answered them, "Sing to the Lord, for He is highly exalted; The horse and his rider He has hurled into the sea."*[6] (Exodus 15:20,21) [emphasis added in bold]

Here she is, identified in Scripture as a prophet and a leader, worshipping the LORD (Yahweh)[7] in victory, leading the others with timbrel (or "tambourine" in some translations) and dance. In singing this song and leading this dance and music, Miriam is more than just an echo of her brother, Moses. Her leadership

6 Exodus 15:20-21.

7 The sacred Name of God, spelled in Hebrew letters Yod-Hei-Vav-Hei, is pronounced as "Yahweh" by some. I have adopted this more common pronunciation for this book, although I suspect it is not entirely accurate. In the Exodus 15 passage just quoted, this name is represented by the word "LORD."

gives all the women of Israel an opportunity to have their own celebration for the mighty, miraculous victory they have just witnessed, where Pharaoh's army of charioteers has just drowned in the sea. Joel Baden has speculated that it might have been "no coincidence" that Miriam steps forward at this time and place to celebrate. The drowning of the Egyptians in the waters of the sea:

> echoes and reverses Pharaoh's decree to drown the Israelite boys in the Nile. The women who saved Moses as a baby have now seen their brave choices pay off in the final elimination of the Egyptians. And who better than Miriam to lead them in celebrating their accomplishments?[8]

Notice that Miriam is described as a **prophet**. A prophet is someone through whom God speaks, someone who consistently hears from Him and releases His revelation into the earth. What did she prophesy? In her song here, she is speaking for God. She is His mouthpiece, telling anyone listening to her song that it was Yahweh, not circumstances, not chance, not some other deity, who destroyed Pharaoh's army.

And this is the primary ministry of the prophet: to interpret events and reveal the truth about God in any given situation. By her song, Miriam interprets recent events, proclaiming the victory and pointing to Yahweh the God of Israel, not to any man or woman, as the true victor over Pharaoh.

This Miriam, a woman who lived more than 3,000 years ago and not under as liberating a covenant as we have now in the blood of Yeshua, shows us that women can be prophets of God and also strong leaders. Men do not have the monopoly on prophetic ministry or on standing in the office of prophet in the earth. Miriam also demonstrates that a prophet is not

8 Joel Baden, "Miriam the Prophetess," My Jewish Learning website, https://www.myjewishlearning.com/article/miriam-the-prophetess/

simply someone who gives personal prophecies or predictions to individuals.

Miriam's position of leadership is honored by a much later prophet, Micah, who recorded hearing these words spoken to him by Yahweh concerning Moses, Aaron and Miriam:

> *My people, what have I done to you, And how have I wearied you? Answer Me. Indeed, I brought you up from the land of Egypt, I redeemed you from the house of slavery,* ***And I sent before you Moses, Aaron, and Miriam.***[9] (Micah 6:3-4) [emphasis added in bold]

Notice that Moses, Aaron, and Miriam are mentioned in the same breath as leaders who were sent to the people of Israel by Yahweh Himself. Together they formed a "bench of three" to lead Israel through the exodus and then the wilderness experience. All three are powerful personalities, who did not always agree with each other, despite the fact that they were brothers and sister.

For those of you who, like me, are well over the age of 60, here is something else encouraging about this Miriam's ministry. Exodus 7:7 says that Moses was 80 years old at the time of the exodus from Egypt. That means that Miriam was either **in her late '80s or early '90s** when she picked up her tambourine to lead the dancing and sang that song of victory! This ministry in her later years reminds us that age is also no barrier to effective ministry (but that would be the subject of another book!).

Miriam the sister of Moses and Aaron is by no means a perfect person, as we will see later in this book. But let's move on to see what we find in the lives of the other Miriams in Scripture. Who are these women named "Miriam"? Why, they are all the Marys of the New Testament.

9 Micah 6:3-4.

Here is an interesting observation about the Miriam we have just read about which I found on a website called "Jewish Women's Archive":

> In the New Testament Miriam's afterlife continues through her name and her deeds. The Greek name Mary is the equivalent of the Hebrew Miriam. In singing a song of deliverance (Luke 1:46–55), in embodying a demonic or diseased condition (Luke 8:2), and in challenging male authorities (Matt 28:10; Luke 24:10; John 20:11–18), the various Marys of the Gospels reflect their namesake.[10]

Questions for reflection, discussion and journaling…

1. *Who are the women you know, either personally or as historical figures, who successfully thwarted the destructive intentions of an authority figure? How did these women accomplish that?*
2. *Is there a person who watches over your neighborhood or your community? What form does their watching take?*
3. *Have you ever been "at the right place at the right time" so that you could intervene in a situation to bring a better result? How did you feel about it afterwards?*
4. *Do you know any older women or men who lead and encourage others by sharing out of the fruit of their spiritual experiences? What about an older believer whose energetic enthusiasm in worship stirs others to greater expression in worship?*

10 https://jwa.org/encyclopedia/article/miriam-bible.

II

MIRIAM OF NAZARETH

Scripture Preview:
Luke 1:26-56
Luke 2:1-7, 19, 51-52

Now that we have looked at the life of Miriam, sister of Moses and Aaron, who are the other Miriams in Scripture? Well, if you put the name "Miriam" into a concordance or a search engine to scan the Scriptures in English, you won't come up with any other Miriams in the Bible. That's because they go by another name: *Mariam* or *Maria* in Greek, and in English, "Mary." **All the Marys of the New Testament were, actually, Jewish women named "Miriam."**

I'm going to say that again: *All the Marys of the New Testament were, actually, Jewish women named "Miriam,"* whom we cherish and love as heroes of the Christian faith.

And isn't it interesting how many of them there were during the time of Yeshua's life on earth? Remember what we learned about that name "Miriam"—a name that spoke of both sweet fragrance and bitter taste. The days when Yeshua (Jesus) walked the earth were bittersweet times indeed. The Jewish people were at relative peace, but their land was occupied by the Romans with their legions of soldiers and high tax levies. So maybe it *was* a good time to name your daughter "Miriam." Or maybe the profusion of Miriams at this time was something that God was doing to lead the people prophetically.

Of course, the most famous Mary, the most famous Miriam in Scripture, is **Miriam, the mother of Yeshua**. And though her life is not the focus of the Gospels, we know enough about her to draw seven wonderful mini-portraits of her. How appropriate, since seven is the number signifying wholeness or completeness in the Bible.

And just to help us disconnect from some of our preconceived notions about this Miriam, we are going to continue to refer to her son Jesus as "Yeshua," which is how you say his name in Hebrew anyway.

Miriam, the Ark of the Presence

Miriam, the yielded "Ark of the Presence," literally carried the Son of God as a human being in her womb. And she did this willingly, voluntarily, and joyfully. In Luke Chapter 1, we read the message the angel Gabriel brings her from God:

> *"Do not be afraid, Mary; for you have found favor with God. And behold,* ***you will conceive in your womb and bear a son,*** *and you shall name Him Jesus. He will be great and will be called the Son of the Most High; and the Lord God will give Him the throne of His father David; and He will reign over the house of Jacob forever, and His kingdom will have no end."* [11] [emphasis added in bold]

11 Luke 1:38.

Now some of us are so familiar with this passage and these names Mary, Jesus, and God that we are missing the flavor of excitement and amazement here. Let's read it again, inserting some Hebraic names:

> *[And Gabriel*[12] *said] "Do not be afraid,* ***Miriam;*** *for you have found favor with* ***Yahweh.*** *And behold, you will conceive in your womb and bear a son. And you shall name him* ***Yeshua.***[13] *He will be great and will be called the* ***Son of El-Elyon.***[14] *And the* ***Lord Yahweh*** *will give him the throne of his father David; and he will reign over the house of Israel forever; and His Kingdom will have no end.* [emphasis added in bold]

The Miriam who heard these words was a teenage girl at the time, betrothed to marry a carpenter named Joseph. Gabriel's message is a heavy-duty message for anyone to receive, especially for one so young! And yet she says yes. Listen to her response of surrender and submission to Gabriel's astonishing message

> *"Behold* ***the bondslave of the Lord;*** *may it be done to me according to your word."* [emphasis added in bold]

This word "bondslave" is significant. I have quoted here from the New American Standard (NASB) translation. Some other English translations use words like "handmaid" or "servant." But the Greek word here is "slave." According to Strong's Greek Lexicon, the underlying Greek doule (pronounced DOO-lay) means a female slave who becomes one either voluntarily or involuntarily.[15] Thayer's Greek Lexicon further defines the

12 Means "God is my strength."
13 Means "the salvation of YHWH."
14 Means "God Most High."
15 Strong's concordance #1399.

metaphorical meaning of this word as a person who is "**devoted to another to the disregard of one's own interests**."[16]

Understand that as a human being, one always has the choice of whether to serve the Lord or not. We are not born His slaves, nor are we "born again" into slavery to Him when we enter into covenant with Yeshua. At some point in our relationship with the Lord, we are given the opportunity to make a deeper commitment than our initial salvation or conversion experience. Some believers may even refer to this as another "conversion" experience, because it profoundly changes one's internal (and eternal) landscape.

The experience I refer to is something that parallels a custom described in Exodus 21:5-6 and Deuteronomy 15:16-17. This is where a Hebrew man or woman who has served a master as a slave for six years is to be set free—unless the slave loves the master so well that the slave wants to be his "servant forever." In that case the master pierces the slave's ear in his doorway as a sign of this change.

Miriam of Nazareth became the bondslave of Yahweh by an act of her own will. No one pierced her ear in a doorway. But she had *already* committed herself and submitted to His will before the angel Gabriel appeared to her, as evidenced by the words she spoke to him in response to the astounding message he gave her from Yahweh.

What does that mean for us? Well, each of us has the opportunity presented to us to live our lives as a "bondslave of the Lord." Some of us might even recall an instance or situation where we sensed the Lord specifically offering us this "bondslave" relationship with Him. What does that mean exactly?

I would describe this relationship as being submitted to "the lordship of the Lord." Very few of us in Western societies

16 THAYER'S GREEK LEXICON, Electronic Database. Copyright 2002, 2003, 2006, 2011.

have lived under the government of an absolute monarch. Some may have lived or perhaps are now living under a dictatorship. Consequently, we don't have a lot of experience to draw on in this regard. But submitting specifically to the lordship of the Lord of lords means that you are committing yourself to absolute obedience to what He tells you to do or to be. He is the boss, and what He says goes in your life. This is a step beyond simply living your life in salvation.

If you don't recall ever specifically committing yourself to this level of obedience, to His absolute lordship, now might be a time to offer that level of commitment to Him. Are you feeling a nudge in that direction?

It's interesting to note that Yeshua Himself was the bondslave of the Father.[17] What does being the bondslave of God mean? How does one walk that out? It means, "Not my will but Yours be done," even in the tight places. We should say, *especially* in the tight places, where it is uncomfortable or undignified—or downright dangerous—to obey His direction.

Accordingly, young Miriam of Nazareth says yes to God's messenger and, by so doing, becomes "Miriam, the mother of Yeshua." She becomes a literal **bearer of the Presence of God, like the Ark of the Covenant** in ancient Israel. The ark was a box about 45 inches long, 27 inches wide, and 27 inches high, constructed of acacia wood and covered in gold. Even the wooden poles used to transport the ark in the centuries before the Jerusalem Temple was constructed were covered in gold. Inside the ark were various artifacts connected with certain miraculous incidents in the history of the relationship between Yahweh and Israel. Among these were:

- the stone tablets with the Ten Commandments, which Moses received on Mt. Sinai;

17 See Philippians 2:7, for example, where Yeshua is referred to as the "doulou" of God. This Greek word, translated commonly as "servant," means actually means "slave."

- the dead almond branch that bore flowers and nuts in one day as a sign confirming Aaron's priesthood; and
- a golden jar containing some of the manna the Israelites received in the desert.

The normal resting place for the ark was in the Holy of Holies, first in the portable sanctuary known as the Tabernacle and later in the Jerusalem Temple. The ark was the closest representation that Israel had to the very personal presence of Yahweh, since they were forbidden by Him to create a statue or idol representing Him. More than being merely a storage place for precious artifacts, the ark was perceived to be *the very presence of God with Israel.*

But Miriam was also more than a "carrier of artifacts." She was a carrier of Emmanuel, "God with us." She was only a young girl at the time of her pregnancy, and you want to say, "How could she possibly understand the significance of what she had agreed to?" But really, what does her age have to do with that? Who among us would have understood the true significance of all that was about to happen with this baby she was carrying?

We know something about the very challenging and stressful situation and conditions surrounding the birth, thanks to the Gospel narratives. We know about Joseph contemplating divorce when he finds out she's pregnant. We know about the census requiring the journey to Bethlehem, the birth in the stable, and the amazing and miraculous visitations to the young child by various beings and personages. We also know about the sudden flight to Egypt when the child was probably less than two years old.

But what was it like for this Miriam to look into the eyes of her little son? What was it like to hear him talk and play as a kid growing up? Hmm. We'll take a look at that a little later in this chapter.

As believers in Yeshua, we too are carriers of the presence—but not quite in the same way. First Corinthians 6:19 says, "*Do you not know that* ***your body is a temple of the Holy*** *Spirit who is in you*?" [emphasis added in bold]

First Corinthians 3:16 similarly says of the body of Christ on the earth, "*Don't you know that you yourselves are God's temple and that* ***God's Spirit dwells in your midst?***" (NIV).[18] [emphasis added in bold] And II Corinthians 6:16 states that we are *"the temple of the living God."* (NIV)

And who is our prototype for this? Yeshua Himself. At a certain point in His ministry, He overturns the tables of the money changers in the Jerusalem Temple. The locals then question His authority for doing this. His answer: "***Destroy this temple*** *and in three days I will raise it up*!" This statement is something that His accusers bring up at His trial. But John, writing about this in John chapter 2, wisely says in verse 21, *"But He was speaking of* ***the temple of His body****."* [emphasis added in bold]

I like to say it this way: *I am a mobile temple of the Holy Spirit.* It's the idea that wherever I go, the presence of God is with me because He is within me. My body is His temple, and I am mobile. I move around, taking Him with me, carrying the potential at all times that He would manifest His Kingdom through me in an outward way. Or indeed that He would manifest Himself to me in the midst of whatever I am living through or walking through at that moment, perhaps even drawing me aside for a refreshing, loving time.

But to walk in this way, we like Miriam of Nazareth need to surrender and submit to the will of God for our own lives. Our reward is to have the joy of the Lord's presence manifesting with us more and more as we interact with Him, just as Miriam did with her son as he grew up and walked in his calling.

18 New International Version translation

Miriam, the Faithful Mother and Wife

And that brings us to a related ministry role in this Miriam's life. I call this her "invisible ministry" as a mother and as a wife. These are the silent years when she is building character and love in her son—and He in her! This is the part of life that is just the daily drip, drip, drip of life. Each day can seem much the same, but every day has its challenges and even its encouragements and delights, especially when that day is lived in the presence of God.

This ministry in Miriam's life touched everyone who came into her sphere of influence. But most of them would not have called it a "ministry." This is where love meets the road of life, where small acts, like performing daily tasks and responsibilities, build a house. Proverbs 14:1 says, "***The wise woman builds her house,*** *but the foolish tears it down with her own hands.*"

And here's another passage from Proverbs:

> ***By wisdom a house is built,*** *And by understanding it is established; And by knowledge the rooms are filled With all precious and pleasant riches.*
> (Proverbs 24:3-4) [emphasis added in bold]

In what sense does anyone "build a house"? Do you have to be a building contractor to do that?

No. The wise woman does and says that which builds up her household, her family, her friends, her community. She builds by her actions, yes, but also and maybe even more so by her words. Words are containers of power—the power to hurt or to heal, the power to build or tear down. Here's what the book of Proverbs says about the words we speak:

> *Death and life are in* ***the power of the tongue,***
> *And those who love it will eat its fruit.*
> (Proverbs 18:21) [emphasis added in bold]

Think of your life as the "house" you're building. If life and death are in the power of your tongue, then the words you speak over your own life matter. They build up or they tear down. And what do they build up or tear down—what blueprint are you following for your life?

Where did the blueprint for Miriam of Nazareth's life come from? It came from **Heaven.** It was written by the will of the Father, and it was delivered in part by at least one angel mentioned in Scripture and in part by people who prophesied to Miriam along the way—people like Elizabeth, Simeon, Anna, shepherds who encountered angels, and the Magi who brought exotic treasures to her son.

And parts of that blueprint for Miriam's life came from Scripture, from the written word of God that Miriam probably learned as a child[19] and the word that she heard in the faith community in which she lived. Of course, her blueprint also came from one particular special individual close to her life: her son. As I said earlier, during these "silent years" about which the Gospel writers say little, Miriam is building character and love in her son, and they are building relationship together.

Some of you are probably thinking, "You mean Yeshua's character wasn't fully formed when He entered this world as a babe?" Yes. Luke tells us that he "***grew in wisdom and stature and in favor with God and with man***." (Luke 2:52 NIV) That's a description of progressive growth in human character, isn't it?

We don't have a lot of specifics about the growth of Yeshua's character as a human being or about Miriam's character as she interacted with him. But during those silent years in the Gospel accounts, she is building a history with Him—living with Him, raising Him as her son, loving Him—and He loving her in the intimate setting of family life.

19 Up to about the age of ten or eleven, girls in that time in Israel were taught to memorize certain portions of Scripture.

During these years what else is Miriam doing? What does her ministry look like? Her ministry consists of running a busy household, taking care of a husband and children, interacting with her neighbors and family members—loving them. When you think of it, how do we know that someone loves us? Maybe one measure of love is action, and the fruit of that action for a mother or father is how the lives of their children turned out.

And by the way, the same dynamic applies to any relationship where someone is a mentor or a teacher/trainer of others. What is the fruit of those relationships? That's the measure of the mentoring or training.

Miriam had a cousin named Elizabeth. In Luke 1:42 Elizabeth exclaims over Miriam, "Blessed are you among women, and blessed is the fruit of your womb!" Yes, the fruit of this Miriam's womb is blessed—not only because He is the Blessed One, the Holy One of Israel, prophesied from of old, but also because He is the blessed fruit of a life that nurtured Him, not only physically but emotionally, socially and spiritually.

The life of Yeshua in the earth is like a seed planted in the womb of Miriam, which grew and matured in hiddenness, in the seeming obscurity of the good soil of her life, cultivated and nourished by a faithful and loving gardener whose ministry was hidden from all but a few pairs of eyes.

All of us have invisible ministries in the earth—things that only God knows we have done which advance His purposes in the earth or in the spirit realm. Who has experienced the love of God through your ministry today? If you stop and consider, you will see that many lives were touched and made better by yours today. Think of the people you spoke to, encouraged, cooked for, cleaned up after, greeted with joy. Think of the lives entrusted to you today, maybe in the workplace, maybe at home or in your neighborhood—people who experienced moments of positive caring in a negative world.

No one sees these moments more clearly than God. And your hiddenness in them is a major training ground for activities we traditionally think of as ministry, because most of these hidden "ministry moments" are never acknowledged or thanked. Most of them flow from a life connected to something other than self-interest or a personal need to be seen or heard in the world.

This hiddenness is a major element contributing to the effectiveness of the ministry of intercession, just to name one example. "Hide and watch" is one of the watchwords of an effective intercessor. If I hear something from the Spirit of God while I'm in prayer, I don't need to go blabbing it all over town so that everyone I tell sees what a "spiritual" person I am. I need only to respond faithfully to that word, praying into it, and watch for it to come to pass in the earth.

Miriam, the Meditative

Miriam of Nazareth is also one of our role models for a practice we might call "meditation." No, I am not talking about the practices associated with Eastern religions like Buddhism or Hinduism, nor am I referring to non-Christian practices like Transcendental Meditation or yoga. The kind of meditation Miriam of Nazareth engaged in was not about emptying the mind but about storing things in one's heart and then thinking about them over and over.

This is a kind of meditation expressed in the Old Testament Scriptures by an ancient Hebrew word "*sichah.*"[20]. Hebrew letters were originally pictographs—that is, they were like little pictures of something. The word *sichah* (which, by the way, is pronounced "see-HAH" with that first H kind of gargled in the back of the throat) begins with the letter Shin, which the rabbis say is the picture of two teeth. The second letter, Yod, looks like our apostrophe but is the picture of a hand, and actually, one

20 Spelled in Hebrew: שיחה.

could argue that this letter represents not just any hand but the hand of God.

The third letter, which is the one that sounds like an H gargled, is the picture of a fence or some say a gateway into a field or yard. And the final letter, Hei, represents an open window through which the wind may blow. In its oldest known form this letter was the picture of a person with his arms raised upward, as if exclaiming, "Behold!" Consequently, this final letter is often associated with what we would call "revelation knowledge" or discovered truth that amazes.[21]

If we put these four pictures together, we might say that the word *sichah* means "to chew on something in a particular field in order to digest the truth God has put there." The short way of saying this is that Hebrew meditation is kind of like a sheep or cow that chews the cud, extracting all the nourishment from it.

This is similar to the English word "ponder," but the Hebrew word is much more vivid in describing the process of meditation. If I meditate or ponder something Hebraically, I turn it over and over in my heart—not frantically or anxiously, but slowly. And each time I do this with the same "cud," I have more and more experience of life and even receive additional revelation from God. This allows me to extract more and more truth, more wisdom and understanding from it, wisdom being the how, when, and where to apply knowledge to construct a course of action—or inaction.

Miriam of Nazareth stores many things about her son in her heart: words the angel Gabriel spoke to her, other words prophesied about him in his infancy and childhood, things he does and says, things that happen to him. During those hidden years of being the faithful wife and mother she ponders them like curious treasures. She remembers the words of Gabriel, the

21 For more information about the specific pictorial meanings of Hebrew letters, see the Hebrew for Christians website, at https://www.hebrew4christians.com/ and click on "Hebrew Letters."

words of Elizabeth, and the words of Simeon. She considers the sudden appearance of shepherds after her son's birth and what they reported about the song of angel choirs.

She marvels at the visit of the *magi* from the East and the gifts they brought. Why those particular gifts? What did they signify? How important this child must be, what a threat he must be, if innocent babes are slaughtered by a jealous and insane monarch in an attempt to stop this child from ever becoming king!

And what about the time he confounded the sages in the Temple at the age of twelve? She gazes at him as he is growing up. She ponders on what she sees and hears, and keeps on chewing on the incidents, the prophecies, the signs—letting all of this shape her soul and character, hoping for understanding—revelation—to invade her meditations (Luke 2:19,51). I said that Miriam of Nazareth was a model for the practice of meditation, as described in Scripture. Far from being a practice where one empties oneself of thought, this type of meditation is about storing words of Scripture, such as the names of God, and other personal words from the Lord in one's heart so that these words transform one's inner climate. That transformation within becomes the foundation for a transformation in one's behavior and speech from the inside out.

Speaking the Scriptures or the phrases that one has received by the Holy Spirit as encouragement over one's life is like chewing the cud. This kind of meditation becomes a repetitive practice pictured in this verse from the Psalms: "*Your word I have* ***hidden within my heart,*** *that I might not sin against You*" (119:11 NKJV). [emphasis added in bold]

Yes, that I might not sin against Him through unbelief—through not believing what He has said and is saying to me concerning my life, the situation I am in, or the life of someone I am related to or concerned about.

This is a practice that is much more than just doing a daily Scripture reading. It is somewhat akin to what some might call "confessing the Word" or "making declarations or decrees" based on the Word of God or based on prophecies or revelations one has received. But whether one ultimately speaks these words aloud or just considers their meaning over and over, this type of meditation is simply pondering those phrases and words that God has highlighted to us or has spoken to us individually.

We'll come back to this subject later when we look at the life of another Miriam, whose actions in relation to Yeshua pictured a related spiritual practice known as "contemplation" or "contemplative prayer."

Miriam, the Intimate Intercessor

Up to this point in Miriam's life as portrayed in the Gospels, we have mostly seen her building a relationship with this son of hers. She is receiving the words of an angel and saying "yes" to a very special invitation to a holy ministry. She makes a home for her son and her husband as a faithful wife and mother. And all along the way she ponders all this, putting together those prophecies, those strange visitations, and her own experience with this child who is the fruit of her own womb and now lives under her roof, growing in favor with God and with man (Luke 2:52).

Then we see an incident that gives us a glimpse of what Miriam discovered during 30 years of living with the son who is now stepping out into the fullness of his earthly ministry. In John chapter 2 we read about a wedding in a village named Cana, where Yeshua, his mother, and some of his newly-called disciples were guests.[22]

In those days it was customary for the wedding feast to last

22 Descriptions of the wedding customs of Yeshua's time: http://blog.adw.org/2014/08/what-were-weddings-like-in-jesus-day/
https://www.myjewishlearning.com/article/ancient-jewish-marriage/

as long as seven days, and in preparation for such a feast, the bridegroom and his father would lay in a great supply of food and drink, especially wine.

Why seven days? Well, maybe some of the reason for the length of the feast had to do with the distance some guests traveled and the custom of hospitality in the ancient world, where there were no Holiday Inns or Denny's.

And then there was the matter of the wedding invitation. You see, even the bridegroom did not know the exact date of his own wedding—not until his father gave him permission to go get the bride. That permission was not given until the bridegroom had paid the bride-price (*mohar* in Hebrew), constructed the bridal chamber (an addition to his father's house), and laid in the requisite supply of food and wine for the feast.

Yes, the guests had invitations of a sort. They knew the couple was betrothed—covenanted unto marriage. But no one actually knew when the wedding feast itself would take place. Only the father of the bridegroom could say when his son could go "steal" his bride in the middle of the night. And when that torchlight parade was made from the bride's house to the site of the wedding feast, that's when the invited guests knew that it was time to celebrate the marriage.

Some invited guests could not easily break away from their daily tasks. Some were notified by servant-messengers that the wedding feast had begun. You can see why the feast might go on and on for several days, as more guests arrived to celebrate with the newlyweds.

And in that ancient Middle Eastern culture where hospitality was extended as a sign of honor to guests, can you imagine what an embarrassment, what a social and cultural disaster it would be if the bridegroom's family ran out of wine at the feast? But that is exactly what happened in John chapter 2. Here's John's account of what happened next:

> *When the wine ran out, the mother of Jesus said to Him, "They have no wine." And Jesus said to her, "Woman, what does that have to do with us? My hour has not yet come." His mother said to the servants,* ***"Whatever He says to you, do it."*** (John 2:3-5) [emphasis added in bold]

Whenever I read this passage, it is for me as if the private relationship between Miriam of Nazareth and her son Yeshua has surfaced for one revealing moment. Consider what she says and why she says it. First, the fact that she is aware of this critical issue in the flow of hospitality of this marriage feast shows that she has a sensitive soul. She anticipates the embarrassment, the social pain of the whole issue—and she wants to remedy it. Does she herself have wine to supply at that moment? No. But she has a son whom she knows at least three things about: 1) he has a compassionate heart that she can appeal to, 2) he has the ability to exercise supernatural power to remedy the situation, and 3) her relationship with him is so strong that he will listen to her plea and act because *she* asked him.

How does she know this? She knows his compassionate heart because she has been observing him and pondering his ways for 30 years. She knows he has the power to remedy the situation. Otherwise, she would not make the request of him. Maybe this Miriam heard an angel or felt the Holy Spirit's nudge, indicating to her that her son could do the kind of miracle here that would save face for this bridegroom in Cana.

But even so, how can she be so sure he can do something? *Because he must have done it before in the privacy of his family setting.* I think (and this is only my personal opinion) he must have "practiced" doing miracles at home. I'm thinking that miracles flowed naturally from the deep relationship Yeshua had with the Father even as he was living a hidden life in Nazareth.

So now at this moment of perceived social need, Miriam knows that Yeshua can save this situation because he has probably done something like it before at home.

And there is yet another dynamic going on here. Miriam is Yeshua's mother. Think about the fourth Commandment: "***Honor** your father and **your mother***" (Exodus 20:12). [emphasis added in bold]It is his *mother* asking this of him, not some other guest at the feast, not one of his disciples, not even the bridegroom or one of his servants. It is this woman, this Miriam whose heart he knows, who bore him under a highly unusual circumstance, who raised him with love—it is *this* woman who is asking him, who is interceding for others who are not yet aware what this son of hers is capable of doing.

It is out of that intimacy of 30 years of living together as mother and child that Miriam intercedes on behalf of a family whose potential shame she wants to avert. And she seals the deal by her confident, if not brash, manner with the servants, even after Yeshua only too clearly does not want to do anything like what she is asking.

Undaunted, she turns to the servants at the feast and says confidently, "***Do whatever He says***!" Kind of like the quintessential Jewish mama, yes? I love this dynamic in the scene. She does not take no for an answer but rather puts some feet to her faith that ultimately, he *will* save the day. Does she presume here? No, she walks in a confidence born of her experience and relationship with him.

It's interesting to note that this episode appears only in John's Gospel. It occurred at a very early point in Yeshua's ministry, at a time when the other three Gospel writers and perhaps their eyewitness sources had not yet become aware of Yeshua. John, on the other hand, was one of the earliest to be called to discipleship. He was probably there at the wedding and maybe knew what had happened with the wine.

But it's even more likely that Miriam herself recounted this story to John in later years. After all, Yeshua entrusted Miriam's care to John from the cross during his agonizing death (John 19:26). Tradition says that, afterward, John lived with her near Ephesus for years while the church in Ephesus grew and grew. Something about this Cana story makes me think that this episode was kind of a "hidden" event at the wedding feast, and only Miriam and Yeshua really knew what went down that day. After all, the point of this miracle was to *hide* the fact that the bridegroom had not provided enough wine, not to make that fact known to the other guests.

Then what does Yeshua do? Well, he does not make a show of praying for a miracle. He simply tells the servants to fill some large wash-pots with water and then draw some of the liquid off and take it to the wine steward for tasting. How did he know what to do? We'll have to ask him someday when he is teaching a master class on John chapter 2. I suspect it had something to do with his maturing relationship as a human being with the Holy Spirit. And even the doing of this water-to-wine miracle had the tender effect of covering the shortcomings of well-intentioned human beings who most assuredly will always need a savior.

And maybe on some level he was looking to the day of his own nuptials in the heavenly Kingdom, when the wine will most assuredly not run out. What a way to begin a miracle ministry! And it began that day because a Jewish mama named Miriam stepped out boldly in loving intercession and would not take no for an answer!

Now before we press on to look at another aspect of Miriam of Nazareth, I am going to take an opportunity to meddle. You'll notice that in the passage quoted above, Yeshua addresses his mother as "woman." I can't tell you the number of sermons and messages I have sat through from well-intentioned men who said that Yeshua's use of this word "woman" was his way of putting the importuning Miriam in her place. Therefore, they interpreted this as if Yeshua was saying, "WOMAN!" because he was highly irritated by her request, so irritated that he was in a verbal sense thrusting her away from him, pushing her aside so to speak.

I think that is about as far from the facts here as one could get in an interpretation of this situation. The word "woman" written in the Greek is actually translated from a word in Hebrew *ishah* (EE-sha) or in Aramaic *attha* (AHT-tha). *Ishah* does mean "woman" in a literal sense. But in a socially intimate moment like this one, it would be used as a term of endearment and familiarity. So picture Yeshua saying "*Ishah*," with a tenderness in his heart mirrored in his eyes. Even though he appears to be turning aside her request, he's not doing it brusquely or with a sense of, "I'll show *you* who's in charge here!"

And while we're on the subject, let's draw another gem from this particular exchange. Notice what Miriam tells the servants: "***Whatever He says to you, do it.***" This is great advice for any day in the life of any person on this planet. *Do whatever He tells you.*

How many times have I failed to do this (yet He forgives me)? How many times have I not done what He tells me to do in His written Word? How many times have I failed to follow through with specific direction I believe He has given me by His Spirit?

Yet the life of a believer is really so simple: *Just do whatever He tells you.* Simple, but not always easy, right?

This episode from the life of Miriam of Nazareth shows us what fruit can come from confident and effective intercession that is based on an intimate relationship with the Lord. He turns your water into wine, takes the ordinary and makes it *sublime*....

And by the way, let's stop and take note of those servants in this story, who do what He says to do. Did you ever stop to think about the faith it took to draw that liquid off those water pots and take it to the *steward* for tasting? They weren't Yeshua's servants, were they? Yet they followed His direction— and apparently kept the secret about how the more-than-enough wine was supplied.

Outstanding. They were ordinary people. So are we. We can walk in that kind of faith also. Just do whatever He tells you. Trust what He says.

Miriam, the Strong Presence at the Cross

Now we shift to a much later scene in the Gospel of John, in the nineteenth chapter. This is a scene that was prophesied in Luke chapter 2, when Yeshua was an infant presented at the Temple in Jerusalem. Miriam was a very new and young mother then, fresh with encounters with angel-seeing shepherds and a newborn son. But when he was presented in the Temple for dedication to the Lord as a firstborn, the prescribed sacrifice having been made, an old man named Simeon came up to Miriam and her husband and began prophesying over the baby.

Simeon had turned to Miriam and said, "*And* ***a sword will pierce*** *even your own soul*" (Luke 2:35) [emphasis added in bold]. In John chapter 19 that day had arrived. She was standing at the foot of a cross on which her beloved son was dying in a horrific and humiliating manner. All of his male disciples, except one—John—had abandoned him. They were watching from a distance, afraid to share his fate. This was something only he could do, and he had to do it alone.

Alone, except for the four loving people mentioned in John's account, who stood at the foot of the cross with him. John gives us details that the other Gospels do not mention because John, "the disciple Yeshua loved,"[23] was right there keeping watch to the very end.

23 John 19:26-27.

And right there with him was Miriam of Nazareth. What did it take for her to stand at the foot of the cross and watch her son suffer for hours? Did she think about all the unfulfilled prophecies over his life, especially the ones about him ascending David's throne? Did she think, "Surely God will rescue him! Surely by some miracle he will come down from that cross, and then everyone will believe he is the Messiah"?

I don't think so. It was, after all, his *detractors* who invited him to come down off the cross, saying they would believe him (Mark 15:30-32). Miriam was not one of *them*.

But what *did* she think about? What kept her there, especially at the very end, as he was drawing his last breaths with increasing difficulty? We don't know how many hours she stood there with John and the other two women. But surely this Miriam had a special measure of grace from the Father. Amazingly the Gospel account does not describe her as wailing or crying. It puts her at the base of the cross as a steady, faithful, loving presence.

We know that her son died for all who witnessed his suffering that day: for the thieves crucified with him, for the disciples who ran away, for the passers-by who mocked him, for the soldiers who drove the spikes through his body—and for the woman who had carried him into this world, who was standing there with loving eyes, probably full of tears, but a steady presence in his ordeal, reminding him visually over and over again why he was dying in this cruel manner.

Once again we glimpse the tender relationship between them in his loving words to her from the cross:

> *When Jesus then saw His mother, and the disciple whom He loved standing nearby, He said to His mother,* ***"Woman, behold, your son!"*** *Then He said to the disciple, "Behold, your mother!" From that hour the disciple took her into his own household.* (John 19:26-27) [emphasis added in bold]

You know, the way we read this passage with our twenty-first century ignorance of what a man suffered as he was dying by crucifixion, we miss the way this really sounded to Miriam and to John's ears as Yeshua spoke this to them. He was near the end, and every breath was an agony, as he had to push up against the place where his feet were spiked to the wood in order to take a breath. He was tiring at this point, about to die of suffocation, unable to draw another breath.

And remember what we said about that word "Woman" he also used in John chapter 2, that word of tender and intimate address? Well, let's make the same substitution here and see what this sounded like to Miriam and John that day:

> *He said to His mother,* ***"Isha........be-hold...... your.......son!"*** *[probably looks toward John.] Then He said to the disciple, "Be-hold...your..... mother!"*

What tenderness in these words. What care, to entrust his mother to the care of the disciple who loved him so well that he stayed there to the end—and the disciple who would live such a long life on the earth that he could take care of Miriam for years and years ahead, until the day that she too would leave the earth.

And her response? She went to live with John (John 19:27). Church tradition says that in her later years they were living in the same area several hours from the city of Ephesus located in modern Turkey.

There were two other Miriams at the cross with Miriam of Nazareth and the disciple John. We'll look at them in later chapters. But what I want us to see is this: Miriam of Nazareth has modeled for us a kind of steadfast love that shows up and shows out at the toughest times, the times when our faith is on trial because of the sufferings of someone we love which we are witnessing. In those times just our steady presence alone without words can be the encouragement our loved one needs to get through that ordeal. There is a time to speak, yes. But there is also a time to be silent (Ecclesiastes 3:7).

That silence is not born of fear or doubt. That silence is a respect for the mysteries we don't understand, tied to the love of God we have known. Just as for Miriam, so for us: It is our experience with God that brings us to a place of standing, and having done all to stand, we remain standing (Ephesians 6:13-14).

Miriam of Nazareth also models for us courage. She stood there with her son, choosing to be numbered among those scorned or mocked for his sake. She did not fear being ostracized by her community of faith or by her neighbors back home or the gossips of Jerusalem. She took care of her son to the end, but he has taken care of her for eternity.

And take note of her reward. We often hear sermons preached about the promise Yeshua makes to the repentant thief on the cross next to him. He is ministering and taking care of human souls to the end. But we hear less often about his provision for Miriam—and for John, for that matter. From the cross, Yeshua joined these two together in a loving bond. Miriam and John are two contemplative souls—two who gazed into the heart of Yeshua and found their true home there.

We too can gaze into His heart and find our true home there. And when we do, we will find kindred spirits also lodged there in that most sacred of hearts. He will see to it that we meet each other!

Miriam, the Pentecostal Believer

We know because we were born this side of the Cross that the cross Miriam stood beneath in John 19 was not the end of the story. We know that Yeshua did not stay in the tomb but was raised to life by the power of the Spirit of God (Romans 8:9-11). From what we have seen about the intimate relationship between Yeshua and his mother, we can only imagine the special reunion they had after his resurrection. That first encounter is a private moment, hidden from us at present.

But something transforming happened to Miriam of Nazareth between the time of the resurrection and the Biblical event we call Pentecost, which happened about 50 days later. Up to this point, Miriam is never shown in Scripture to be a disciple of her son, never a direct part of his itinerating ministry group. But after Yeshua instructs his disciple in Acts chapter 1 to wait in Jerusalem until they are "endued with power from on high," we read this:

> *"These all with one mind were continually devoting themselves to prayer, along with the women, and* ***Mary the mother of Jesus,*** *and with His brothers."*[24] [emphasis added in bold]

Thus on a Biblical feast day called *Shavuot* in Hebrew and *Pentecost* among the Greek-speaking Jews,[25] Miriam and her family members were among the 120 gathered in an upper room of a house in Jerusalem when this happened:

> *Suddenly there came from heaven a noise like a violent rushing wind, and it filled the whole house where they were sitting. And there appeared to them tongues as of fire distributing themselves, and they rested on each one of them. And* ***they were all filled with the Holy Spirit and began to speak with other tongues,*** *as the Spirit was giving them utterance.*[26] [emphasis added in bold]

24 Acts 1:14.
25 Jewish Encyclopedia article, entitled "Pentecost" (1906 edition).
26 Acts 2:2-4.

Miriam, like all the others present, is filled with the Holy Spirit. Tongues of fire rest on Miriam, and she speaks in tongues, like all the others. And remember that Paul tells us that 500 believers saw Yeshua in one of his post-resurrection appearances. But only 120 were there in that upper room in Jerusalem, waiting for what He promised them.

Miriam was one of those who received the promise that day. Miriam is among the first Pentecostal believers in history! What does that mean for us today? It means that if *she* needed to be "endued" or endowed with power from on high, so do we. It means that if she could be immersed in the Holy Spirit of God, so can we. How did that happen for her? By her "doing what He said to do." He told all of His disciples to wait until they received this powerful experience, and **Miriam followed His directions.**

She is an example of the faithful, obedient believer who presses in to receive more of God, who believes what she hears from God and acts on it in faith. If we follow her example, who knows how deep we might go with Him? Who knows how supernatural our lives might be, even on this side of Heaven?

This wonderful Miriam, a mother to us in faith, is seldom talked about in Protestant, Evangelical, or Charismatic Christian circles, except at Christmas time. It's almost as if we don't want to get too close to her, lest we fall into the "errors" we think we see among the Catholics and Orthodox believers who make so much of her, in our view. I hope you see from what I've written about her here that her life has depths of treasures for all of us to discover and ponder.

Questions for reflection, discussion and journaling…

1. *How do you think you would react if an angel suddenly appeared to you?*

2. *How would you describe your own relationship with God or with Yeshua? Have you ever presented yourself to Him in prayer as His "servant" or "bond-slave"?*
3. *How aware are you that you are an "ark," a carrier of the presence of God?*
4. *Is being a faithful spouse and/or a parent who raises children (either natural children or spiritual ones) actually a ministry honoring the Lord by imitation? Isn't part of God's ministry to us one of parenting us?*
5. *Miriam of Nazareth leveraged her relationship with her son at Cana to obtain a certain result for others. Do you think that a deepening personal relationship with God would change the way you approach prayer? What about the results of your prayer—would they improve?*
6. *Taking this a step deeper, what if you set yourself to live out these words the next time you face a decision point in life: "Do whatever He tells you"? In order to do this, you will need to practice using your spiritual ears and eyes to perceive what He is communicating to you, right?*
7. *How has your view of Miriam of Nazareth changed after reading this chapter?*

III

MIRIAM OF MAGDALA

Scripture Preview:
Luke 8:2
John 19:26
John 20:1-18

Miriam of Magdala—Mary Magdalene—is an interesting but somewhat overlooked figure in the Gospels. We do know some additional bits of information about her from early church writings outside of Scripture. She is the kind of woman that legends are written about. But we don't have to access any of those legends to draw a compelling portrait of this Miriam from the Gospels.

"Magdalene" refers to the fact that she came from Magdala, a town in northern Israel on the Sea of Galilee. Magdala (current name "Migdal") was a prosperous fishing village, known also for its synagogue, which was unearthed in recent years. Yeshua is said to have preached in synagogues throughout the Galilee area and probably also preached in this synagogue, which was just a few miles from Capernaum, his base for ministry.

Miriam, Set Free by the Messiah

Luke 8:2 refers to Miriam of Magdala as someone from whom Yeshua or His disciples had cast out seven demons. Her name appears in this list of women who traveled with Yeshua and his disciples:

> *The twelve were with Him, and also some women who had been healed of evil spirits and sicknesses:* ***Mary who was called Magdalene, from whom seven demons had gone out,*** *and Joanna the wife of Chuza, Herod's steward, and Susanna, and many others who were contributing to their support out of their private means.* [emphasis in bold]

The Gospels do not give us an account of the initial encounter between this Miriam and Yeshua. We do know from Mark 16:9 that Yeshua himself cast out the seven demons. But we don't know whether those demons were cast out in the synagogue, in the marketplace, or on the seashore. And we don't know from the text how living with those demons had affected her behavior and hence her life.

There is a tradition in the Catholic Church that gained prominence in the sixth century that paints her life as a repentant prostitute—or at least as a loose woman whose life was reformed by Yeshua's ministry. Some have speculated over the centuries that she is the unidentified woman in Luke 7 who washes the feet of Yeshua with her tears and wipes them with her hair while he is reclining at table in a rich Pharisee's house.

That's possible, if she was living a life of great sin before she was freed from those demons. Certainly, those who have been forgiven much (and who have been set free from much) love much. But it is interesting to note that in the Eastern Orthodox Church, she is revered solely as a saintly, servant of God, without reference to a former "bad girl" lifestyle. It makes me think they didn't buy the story that she was ever a prostitute. More recently, some bible scholars have speculated that she might have been a wealthy widow, though there's no specific evidence of that in the Gospels.

Whatever she was, one thing is certain. After getting free from those demons, she joined the band of disciples and served in Yeshua's ministry along with several other women named in the Gospels. I guess you could say she "did a 180"—meaning she turned the direction of her life completely around, turning away from the influence of the demonic kingdom that had been troubling her and turning towards the Kingdom of Heaven which Yeshua preached and demonstrated.

It is kind of odd that she travels with this group of men. She is not described anywhere in Scripture as being or having been the wife of anyone. She appears to have been an unmarried woman at the time she traveled with the disciples. That would seem to indicate that after her deliverance from those demons, she had nowhere to return to. She may as well have been an outcast or one who did not want to return into the environment in which she had lived.

It is also interesting to note that Yeshua let her travel with them, unlike the mad man of Gadara, from whom Yeshua cast out demons who described themselves as "Legion." That man, sometimes referred to in Christian literature as the "Gadarene demoniac," begged Yeshua to let him travel with the band of disciples. But Yeshua told him to go testify to his neighbors about his deliverance instead. Apparently he didn't give the same direction to Miriam of Magdala.

How does this relate to us today? I speak as one who came to saving faith in Yeshua as an adult, in actual fact at about the age of 30. I was not a prostitute or a drug addict or anyone viewed as one of the common outcasts of our modern society.

But like Miriam of Magdala, I "did a 180"—turned 180 degrees in the opposite direction from where I was going in life. After my salvation experience, I found myself drawn like a magnet to things like Bible reading, prayer and church meetings—things I could have cared less about before I accepted my salvation.

I found also that other things, like my career ambitions, that had had a big place in my life and seemed so important to me had suddenly lost their charm. Most of all, I found myself drawn to the ***person*** of Yeshua, first by what I read in Scripture and then by a series of powerful encounters with Him by the Holy Spirit. My life was never the same. My career path, my social life—everything about me changed direction.

Can you identify with this? Miriam of Magdala found someone who was worth leaving everything behind for. She found someone so worth serving and loving that it gave her own life purpose and meaning to be associated with him. And isn't that what we long for—love and significance?

Yeshua is someone who, the longer you know him, the more the purity of his character hits you between the eyes. And you think despairingly, "How could I ever measure up to him? How could I ever be a friend or companion of his?" But then once again, he assures you of your acceptance, of the righteousness you have because of His blood shed for you. The bond of His love for you never breaks or grows thin. It is new every morning (Lamentations 3:22-24).

Miriam, the Faithful Disciple of Messiah

And thus it was for Miriam of Magdala. As I said, this Miriam's initial intersection with the ministry of Yeshua is not recorded in specifics. But from a certain point onward, it is clear in the Gospels that she traveled with Yeshua and his male disciples. If Miriam had been a married woman or the relative of any of the male disciples, she would likely have been identified that way in the text. The fact that she is identified by her town of origin would seem to say that she was a single, never-married woman.

Do you understand how "off the charts" that made her? Traveling around with this group of men was almost scandalous in the time and place in which she lived. Probably the only thing that made it less than a scandal was the fact that a small group of married women (possibly wealthy widows) also traveled with them (Luke 8:3). But apparently Miriam measured her situation this way: She had nothing more to lose reputation-wise and everything to gain by attaching herself to this mobile ministry.

Reading between the lines a bit, we could suppose that she is just as much a disciple of Yeshua as the men were. What did disciples of famous rabbis do in Yeshua's day? Well, the relationship between rabbis and their *talmidim*[27] in Yeshua's time was pretty well-defined by tradition. The disciples of the rabbi certainly worked hard at times to serve the needs of the group (and especially of the rabbi) as they traveled with him.

But their primary focus was to study the rabbi himself. They watched how he interacted with all kinds of people—with men, women, children, elderly, rich, poor, sick, Gentile, religious, etc. They studied his way of speaking, his gestures, his prayers, and the blessings he said over daily tasks and events. They listened to his teachings and answered his many questions posed to them.

And they did all this because their goal, their objective, was to become "just like the rabbi." A rabbi is a sage, a person who knows how to live "the text and the tradition" wisely and well before God. The "text" he lives is the Holy Scriptures (primarily the Torah)[28], and the "tradition" in Yeshua's time included much orally-transmitted tradition about how the text should be lived.

27 Talmidim is a Hebrew word that has been translated "disciples."
28 Torah is comprised of the books of Genesis, Exodus, Leviticus, Numbers and Deuteronomy.

A well-trained disciple was one who only *did what he saw his rabbi doing and said what he heard his rabbi say.*

Consequently, as Yeshua himself put it, a disciple, when he is fully trained, will be *just like his rabbi* (Luke 6:40).

Now Yeshua was not exactly a traditionalist, as famous rabbis go. In actual fact, the very way he chose his disciples and the particular people to whom he offered discipleship was so unconventional that it undoubtedly drew the wrong kind of attention. Consider that he had among the Twelve a former tax collector (Matthew) and a political extremist (Simon the Zealot). He was also derisively called a "friend of publicans and sinners" (Matthew 11:18-19 KJV), as if this was evidence that he himself was not righteous enough to be called a rabbi.

But like the few famous rabbis of his day who were considered to be the "best of the best," Yeshua did gather disciples to himself and did take them with him as he itinerated from village to village. These disciples lived with him, ate with him, walked dusty roads with him, camped with him—all the while listening to his conversations and casual remarks, studying his manner and his actions, so that they could imitate the way he lived before God and man.

And Miriam of Magdala was one of these who traveled with him. Accordingly, Miriam was likely there for the private sessions, where Yeshua would explain the parables that he had spoken publically in his teachings to the multitudes. She saw him do miracles—healing the sick, multiplying food, raising the dead—up close and personal.

She was a disciple too, though not numbered among the Twelve. We have the idea, many of us, that Jesus had only twelve disciples. But in truth, if you read the Gospels carefully, at one point in his ministry he had about 70 others beside the Twelve, whom he sent out on ministry assignments after they had spent some time with him. And of course, there were those women I mentioned earlier, including Miriam of Magdala.

The Twelve are kind of the inner circle, the lives into which Yeshua poured personal attention and training more than the others who joined with him later. They were his ministry team and his support staff. Those of us who read the Gospels without having a cultural background in the traditions of that day do not see the dynamic of the rabbi-disciple relationship of that time. For example, most of us don't see the cultural reasons why someone would walk away from their family business, as Peter and Andrew did, because an itinerating rabbi said simply, "Follow me" (Matthew 4:18-20). And most of us don't understand the purpose of discipleship in that culture. (Maybe I should write a book about that!)

But here's what gets my attention. The way I see it, God took Miriam's past, which because of those troubling demons had to have been pretty awful whether she was a prostitute or not, and actually turned it to His advantage! I know I'm reading between the lines here, but it seems to me that for whatever reason, she felt she could not go back to her life in Magdala after she no longer had those seven demons.

And because of that, she now had a front-row seat for some of the most astounding events ever to occur on the face of the earth. Isn't that just like God to take the awful parts of a person's life and turn them into something really good (Genesis 50:20)?

Here's the great news about that: He'll do something similar for you and for me. He will take all the ick in our pasts and redeem it. "Redeem" does not mean simply "wash it clean" or "get rid of it." No, God is so much better than that! He will actually take our stuff, even our bad stuff, and recycle it, or as we would say in the twenty-first century, **repurpose** it. Maybe that takes the form of past mistakes becoming the subject for turnaround testimonies. Or maybe something good you used to do a long time ago that you never enjoyed doing suddenly becomes a useful experience today in a ministry context.

I recently had an opportunity to help a Christian businessman navigate a complex legal transaction he was doing with another attorney. Decades ago, before I had any relationship with God, I used to work on a legal team that handled those kinds of complex legal transactions. I never thought I would be doing anything like that again. But never say "never" with God. Something from my past was repurposed by God for His advantage—and mine.

And the bad times—not just the times when we have sinned greatly, but the times when we didn't know how we were going to make it through something—those times He will often repurpose in surprising ways also. It's as if the wounds we have been healed of inside our hearts are now lined with the gold of Heaven. And it is the comfort we received through that healing process that we use to comfort others who cross our paths in the oddest ways (II Corinthians 1:3-4). Yes, He uses all of that to weave the tapestry of our lives.

He used Miriam's past to weave a vastly different future. He took what may have looked to many as an absolute barrier to ministry and repurposed it to open doors of effectual ministry for Miriam of Magdala.

Miriam, the Strong and Faithful Friend

In the previous chapter we saw that Miriam of Nazareth was one of the few friendly faces gathered at the foot of the Cross, as Yeshua hung there, dying. The disciple John was also there with her.

And so was Miriam of Magdala (John 19:25). Here is another strong Miriam who risks arrest, who risks ridicule and ostracism by publicly standing with this Man who is being executed as a political and religious criminal, rejected by Jews and Gentiles alike. Here is a woman who seems not to care one whit for her own reputation.

Maybe that's because her reputation had been shredded long ago. But I think she is there because of her love that abandoned everything else for Him. He is the one who pulled her out of the mire and hell of her demon-possessed past. He is the one who accepted her as part of His traveling band of disciples. He is the one whom she had the privilege to study as He preached His message, healed the sick, forgave the sinner, and fended off critics until the *kairos*[29] moment of His arrest and trial, when He opened not his mouth in self-defense.

Who would *not* love Him? I often say that to the Lord. His heart is like a magnet drawing in the human soul. Everything about His character and nature is so wonderful. Words are not big enough, powerful enough to express what He is really like. He is Miriam's "all in all" (Colossians 3:11). He completely fills the screen of her vision. Nothing else matters.

Nothing else matters but to be a faithful and strong support to him in this time of his ultimate trial. Did she understand what he was really doing? Did she think he would come down from the Cross in some magnificent miraculous display? I don't know. And if he particularly addressed her from the cross, those words are not recorded in the Gospels. I can't imagine he ignored her, though.

How does this relate to us? We can't stand at the foot of the Cross and by our very witness there bring comfort to Him like she did—or can we? There is an ancient spiritual practice[30] of putting yourself into the scriptural narrative you are reading. If you are reading an account of the crucifixion, for example,

---

29 Kairos is a Greek word for "time," as in an opportune moment, the right time for the accomplishment of a crucial action.

30 Ignatius of Loyola (1491-1556) practiced a spiritual discipline of imagining himself fully within a story from the Gospels. He advocated this as a way to receive truths from Scripture beyond mere theological discussion. If you think of yourself as an onlooker in a gospel story, you can observe what the day felt like and smelled like. You watch what the disciples and others are doing. And above all, you watch Yeshua (Jesus): how he moves, the look on his face, in his eyes, what he does. You hear him say the words from Scripture, and you may also hear him say something directly to you—or just look at you in the crowd. This is a very powerful way to read Scripture and can lead to powerful spiritual encounters with the Lord.

you can locate your own heart by considering where you would likely be standing. Would it be on one of the surrounding hills, watching at a distance? Would you have been a passerby? One of the disciples hiding from the law? One of the festival-goers, preparing the Passover feast for that evening?

Or would you have been like Miriam, standing near Him, because your heart would not let you stay away from him in his time of trial? It takes a lot of strength to do that. It takes a strong heart to stay hour after hour, looking on him who has been beaten almost beyond recognition (Isaiah 52:14 & 53:3) and now is dying a horrific, tortured death, especially when you love him.

Some say it was love that kept the Christ on the cross. But it surely was also love that kept John and the two Miriams at the foot of the Cross to the very end. This reminds me of the words of a worship song, a love song to Jesus, written and sung by Darlene Zschech and Ron Kenoly that I have loved for years, entitled *You Are.*[31] When I sing this song to Him, I am saying that He is the love of my life—my everything.

I like to sing this song to Him and remind myself that no matter what is going on in my life, good or bad, He is my focus. He is my "true north." He was surely "true north" for Miriam of Magdala. It is true: she who has been forgiven much loves much. (Luke 7:47)

Miriam, Heart of a Servant

We know that the gospel story does not end at the Cross. It does not end at the tomb. But in the Scriptures, the last portrait we have of Miriam of Magdala is on Resurrection Day. Early on that day she would learn "the rest of the story."

Just as she was faithful in life, Miriam was prepared to be faithful in death. She and at least one other woman had

31 © Warner Chapel Music.

accompanied the men who put Yeshua's body in Joseph of Arimathea's tomb on the day he died:

> *Joseph bought a linen cloth, took Him down, wrapped Him in the linen cloth and laid Him in a tomb which had been hewn out in the rock; and he rolled a stone against the entrance of the tomb.* ***Mary Magdalene and Mary the mother of Joses were looking on*** *to see where He was laid.* (Mark 15:46-47) [emphasis added in bold]

What followed was at least one or perhaps two days of Sabbath, when no work could be done. Scholars have some debate about this, but Passover began at sundown on the day Yeshua died. The first day of Passover was a Sabbath (Leviticus 23: 5-7). It is likely that the day after the first day of Passover fell on a regular weekly Sabbath. Thus it was that on the third day after the crucifixion the women could return to the tomb and finish their preparations of the body resting there.

What was normally done for a Jewish burial at that time was that certain spices and herbals, including aloes and sweet smelling myrrh, were scattered on and packed around the body. John 19:39 tells us that Joseph of Arimathea, a wealthy man, bought both an expensive linen burial cloth for Yeshua's body as well as 75 pounds of myrrh and aloes.

Normally that amount of myrrh and aloes would have been enough to bury 100 men! But according to the historical records about other men of high esteem buried at the time, the more one esteemed the dead man, the greater the quantity of these expensive materials that were spread in his burial. They would have been arranged around the body covered in a cloth which was not wound horizontally like Egyptian mummies were but wound vertically from head to toe, like a "U" set on its side. The body would rest within that U-shape of linen cloth that covered both front and back sides of the body.

Yeshua died a few hours before sunset. Therefore the preparation of his body was somewhat hasty and may not have been completed. Or perhaps the women who came at dawn on the third day came out of respect to make sure everything had been done right.

Whatever the reason, Miriam arose and accompanied several women who were returning to the tomb with spices.(Mark 16:1). Understand that she is not going there because she believes he will rise from the dead—she's going to finish preparing his dead body. This is an act of loving service. All four Gospels mention her doing this.

But something unexpected happens. Mark 16:9 says that after His resurrection, Yeshua **first** appeared to Miriam of Magdala. Why was that? Why *this* Miriam? I think it was because she was at the right place at the right time, yes—but also because of her grieving heart and because of the tender heart of the Lord.

John's Gospel gives us a longer account of what transpired outside the tomb. At first Miriam sees that the stone has been rolled away and the body is gone, and she supposes that someone has taken the body away (John 20:2). She informs Peter and John of this, who were apparently on their way to the tomb to pay their respects. They looked into the tomb and saw only the burial cloth and the strips of linen that had been used to bind Yeshua's hands and feet together in burial, plus a linen cloth which, tellingly, had been "rolled up in a place by itself," perhaps as if someone had thoughtfully dealt with it (John 20:7).

The disciples go back to where they were staying. But Miriam stands outside the tomb weeping. I want you to picture her heart at that moment. This wonderful person who had freed her in every way from a hellish existence had died a tortured, dishonoring death, suffering in front of her eyes just a few days ago. And now apparently this great insult—someone has opened the grave and made off with his corpse.

Miriam is not recorded in the Gospels as "weeping" during the crucifixion. I don't think that means she didn't cry at all. I think it means that she was not loudly wailing as he died. But here at the empty tomb, it's like the last straw, and she just lets it out. Then, kind of like she can't believe the body is really not there, she stoops and looks into the tomb again.[32]

Now she sees two angels, one at the place where Yeshua's head had lain and the other where his feet would have rested. She may not have realized at the moment that they **were** angels. They ask her why she is weeping. And she answers that someone has taken away "my Lord" and she doesn't know where He is now laying. (John 20:12-13)

She turns to leave, and outside the tomb she sees Yeshua without recognizing him. She was not expecting to see him standing there alive, was she? He addresses her with that Hebrew word we've talked about, *isha*, which is translated "woman." It's that tender word of address used in conversation with someone familiar.

> ***"Woman, why are you weeping?*** *Whom are you seeking?" Supposing Him to be the gardener, she said to Him, "Sir, if you have carried Him away, tell me where you have laid Him and I will take Him away."* (John 20:15)

Notice that she's ready to rebury his dead body! Almost sounds like she would have carried it away herself. But then the moment comes. He says to her, "Miriam!" And she answers, *"Rabboni!" Rabboni*[33] is a Hebrew word that means "my rabbi."

32 Notice she had looked, but now she looks again and sees more—the angels. This is a good practice for all of us whenever we are having any kind of encounter with heavenly beings, to look and look again. Daniel, Ezekiel, Zechariah and John did this also. Examples of this in Daniel: 7: 4, 6, 7, 13, 21. In Ezekiel: 1:4; 2:9; 8:2,7,10; 10:1, 9; 37:8; 44:1. In Zechariah: 1:18, 2:1, 5:1, 6:1. In Revelation: 4:1; 6:2, 5.

33 Pronounced "rah-bo-NEE"

It's the word a disciple uses to address his own rabbi, a term of great respect and familiarity, almost like saying "my dear rabbi." Miriam's use of it at this moment shows her close connection with him and actually is more evidence that she saw herself as His disciple.

Think about this. That is a huge turn of events to take in. He is alive! It's so wonderful... But wait, there is another big change coming. In verse 17 of John 20, Yeshua says something that brings their relationship with each other to a far different level:

> *"Stop clinging to Me, for I have not yet ascended to the Father; but go to My brethren and say to them,* ***I ascend to My Father and your Father,*** *and My God and your God."* [emphasis added in bold]

"***Stop clinging to Me***"—apparently she is holding on to Him for dear life (wouldn't you?). And does she realize what He's saying—that He stopped here on His way to Heaven to make Himself known to her? But the purpose of that stop was not merely a personal one. He is **commissioning** her, assigning her a task to make known what she is now witnessing and to preach the "rest of the story"—that He is ascending to present Himself to the Father, whom He identifies also as "your Father" and to God as "My God and your God."

In other words, Miriam is now in the family of God, and Yeshua, though clearly speaking as Son of God in this passage, remains also Son of Man, even after his ordeal of death and his glorious resurrection. Furthermore, Miriam is now to tell all of this to the brethren, including the two male disciples who looked and left, missing this encounter.

I want to stop here a moment and make a special point. Notice that Yeshua is giving this task of sharing the message of this encounter, truly the good news of the gospel, to a **woman**. This is such a huge departure from the culture of the time, and even something that flies in the face of the traditional practices of some churches. Ask yourself: If Miriam of Magdala showed up on a Sunday morning in some of our churches, would she be allowed to preach from the pulpit?

Women who have had dramatic encounters with Yeshua, whose lives have been turned around by their continuing vital relationship with Him, are routinely kept away from sharing on a Sunday morning in many churches. But that doesn't mean they were not commissioned by Him or have no place to share their story, does it?

With those words from Yeshua, Miriam of Magdala has become an evangelist. We traditionally think of evangelists as folks who bring the gospel message of salvation to the unsaved. But the Greek word *evangel* simply means "gospel." Miriam has been commissioned to bring some very good news, some *gospel*, to those disciples hiding out in Jerusalem. Miriam indeed has been commissioned to bring the piece of the gospel message that makes all the rest of it come alive: ***the resurrection of Christ.***

What was it that Paul said? *"If Christ has not been raised, then our preaching is vain,* ***your faith also is vain"*** and *"If Christ has not been raised, your faith is worthless;* ***you are still in your sins"*** (I Corinthians 15:14,17) [emphasis added in bold]. The resurrection is the absolute centerpiece of the basis for faith in Yeshua, the linchpin that holds everything else about the believer's life together.

And note that Yeshua gives the preaching of this important fact to a woman—to our Miriam. Yes, it was through a woman (Eve) that the human race fell. But there's something redemptive about a woman being the first eyewitness of the resurrected Savior.

I have a lot more to say about this. But I'll save that for my final mini-portrait of this Miriam. For now, let me just take note of the fact that because Miriam is serving the Lord out of her loving heart, she is at the right place at the right time to encounter Him. You and I can encounter Him also by being faithful to serve Him.

I'm thinking of times when I was simply taking care of basics at home or at church, when suddenly His presence came. I know this is not an unusual occurrence for Him. If you've read the classic book, *Practicing the Presence*, you know that Brother Lawrence (a seventeenth-century Carmelite monk) often had encounters with the Spirit of the Lord while he was washing dishes or going about menial tasks at the monastery.

Miriam of Magdala was serving the Lord directly by going to the tomb with the other women that morning. But it was her heart of love borne of relationship that caused her to **remain** at the tomb in tears. Every one of us has the opportunity to build an intimate history with Him every day. Each one of us can be as close to Him as we want to be. Our closeness with Him is not determined or pre-determined by Him. It is a product of **our own** desires and actions.

For us, that might be showing up faithfully to prayer daily or to read the Word of God, using these spiritual disciplines as doorways into conversation with the Lord, heart to heart and spirit to spirit. Or it could be faithfully serving others in daily life in a way that brings Him glory, seeing His face in the faces of those you serve.[34] If you make yourself available to Him, don't be surprised if one day you hear His voice giving you an assignment. It could come as a gentle nudge or idea that you're thinking was not you. Or it could come as a strong and booming internal voice, full of authority, which directs you to do something that

34 Consider this passage: "Whatever you do, do your work heartily, as for the Lord rather than for men, knowing that from the Lord you will receive the reward of the inheritance. It is the Lord Christ whom you serve." Colossians 3:23-24.

brings honor to the Lord's name. And yes, it could come as an audible voice from the unseen realm. I have known several people who have actually had this type of experience, though it is not common.

However it comes to you, accept the assignment He gives you. If you are faithful in very small things, He will give you bigger assignments.[35]

Miriam, Preacher of the Good News

What was the assignment that Yeshua gave Miriam on that Resurrection morning? Well, His immediate word to her was to "go tell My brethren…." He entrusted a message to her to deliver to the men with whom he had been living and traveling for almost three years.

"Wait," you're thinking, "I thought *those* guys were the evangelists. I thought *those* guys were the ones with the big ministry assignments. *Those* are the guys God chose to bring the gospel message, right?"

Not exactly. Yes, those guys were also chosen. But right there in John 20 we see the Lord giving His first post-Resurrection commissioning for ministry to a **woman**—to this Miriam.

And what is her response? She faithfully delivers the message He entrusts to her. John 20:18 says that she came to the disciples, announcing, proclaiming to them that she had actually seen the Lord and that He had given her a message for them, which she then delivered to them.

And what was *their* response? Luke reports that "these words appeared to them as nonsense, and they *would* not believe" (24:11). Astounding. These are the men who saw Him raise the dead, who heard Him prophesy to them about His own resurrection. And now when Miriam (and indeed the other two women who went to the tomb with her that day) gave her

35 See Luke 19:17.

personal, eyewitness testimony, they *would* not receive it!

I am belaboring this point here for two reasons. First, I want you to see that even when God Himself sends someone like Miriam on an errand, that errand does not always appear to end successfully. Wow, has that ever happened to *you?* You are sure God has told you to take some particular action or to give someone a certain message or teaching, or maybe do a particular act of kindness for someone. And yet it seems to fall flat on its face, seems entirely unsuccessful—to the point where you begin to wonder whether it really was God's direction to do that thing.

That has certainly happened to me at times. And when it does happen, in humility I recall people like Miriam of Magdala who actually received a direct visit from God to do something, and yet when they did what He requested, nothing seemed to come of it. You know it's not a wasted effort on Miriam's part—or on God's part, for that matter. Often it seems that we humans need to hear something multiple times before we begin to accept it as true. So in that economy of faith, Miriam made a deposit by her testimony. She told them one important thing, one time. Later when a few disciples on the road to Emmaus encounter the risen Lord also, another deposit is made. Notice that *that* deposit doesn't move the other disciples to action either when it is shared!

Finally, as the disciples remain in Jerusalem rather than travel to Galilee as the Lord had directed them (Matthew 26:32), He simply appears to a group of them in the evening, not even bothering to unlatch the locked door by His entry. They have Miriam's message standing right in front of them.

The other point I would like to make here is that Miriam by no means let the fact the men did not believe her stop her from giving others her testimony. We hear nothing more about this Miriam in the Scriptures after the Gospels. But that does not mean she vanished into obscurity. She is recorded in early

Church tradition as having ministered the gospel all over the Mediterranean region for the rest of her life. She may have traveled as far west as Marseilles, France.

Today some would probably describe her ministry as "apostolic." What is an apostle? An apostle was originally a military designation referring to one who brings a foreign culture to establish it in a newly conquered territory on the earth. In the New Testament we might say that an apostle is one who has had a personal encounter with the risen Christ and is commissioned by Him to demonstrate and establish the culture of Heaven in the community of believers.

Miriam of Magdala preached the gospel of the resurrection with the authority of an eyewitness to a pagan culture in a time when travel was dangerous even for men. Her unconventional life path was something the Lord used to His advantage to spread the Kingdom of Heaven in the earth. In her ministry we can see the possibility that the Lord would call us also to preach and to testify of the living Lord, out of our own encounters with Him.

Questions for reflection, discussion and journaling...

1. *What specific things in your life—habits, addictions, fears, traumas, etc.—have you been freed from through your relationship with Yeshua or with God?*

2. *A disciple in Yeshua's day "did what he saw his rabbi doing and said what he heard his rabbi saying." Who is it that you are imitating?*

3. *Here's a challenge: set aside a time to read one of the gospel accounts of the crucifixion. Now read it slowly again, letting your imagination take you into the scene being described. Who are you? Where are you? What are you seeing, hearing, experiencing? What are you feeling?*

4. *Most women, even in contemporary Western societies, still engage in menial household tasks and take care of the physical and emotional needs of others. Are you able to see this as a ministry? What if you saw the common tasks of your daily life as co-laboring with the Lord, being His hands and feet in the earth?*

5. *Can you picture a physical encounter with the living Yeshua? What would you feel if He suddenly appeared to you in the room where you're sitting? What would you do? What would you say?*

6. *Do you really believe in the resurrection of Yeshua?*

7. *Before reading this chapter, did you ever think of any woman in Scripture as an evangelist or an apostle? Do you think it is important to give people in public ministry titles like "evangelist" or "apostle"?*

IV

MIRIAM OF BETHANY

Scripture Preview:
Luke 10:38-41
John 12:1-9

Now we come to Miriam of Bethany. This is the Miriam who is the sister of Lazarus and Martha. Like Miriam of Magdala, this Miriam seems to be unmarried. We don't know how old she is, but it is a curious thing that both she and her sister are unmarried. As we go along through the Scriptures that mention this Miriam, I will try to point out the clues we have in the text as to why this might be so.

Miriam, Martha, and Lazarus are siblings—brother and sisters. Their parents are never mentioned, so we may assume they are dead. Miriam lived with Martha and Lazarus in the village of Bethany, a suburb as we would say of Jerusalem. It is located on the eastern slope of the Mount of Olives, about two miles from the old wall of the city.

The name "Bethany" can be translated and interpreted at least two ways. Its literal meaning is "**House of Dates**," as in date palms. Have you ever tasted a date? The sweetest dates are the

Medjool, which come from Israel and several other countries in the Middle East. In Yeshua's time, women used a syrup prepared from these dates as their primary sweetener, like we would use honey or maple syrup.

Accordingly, Bethany has an association with sweetness. But it was also the site of a hospice run by a colony of ascetics.[36] Literary evidence from one of the Dead Sea Scrolls describes a hospice in Bethany for the unclean, such as lepers, as well as the destitute. Maybe that gave rise to an alternative interpretation of the name "Bethany" as "**House of Misery**."

Note that the road into Jerusalem went right past Bethany as it began its half-circle around the Mount of Olives.

Who are Lazarus, Martha and Miriam?

In the day when Martha, Lazarus and Miriam lived on the earth, it would not have been so unusual for a man under the age of 30 not to have a wife. Lazarus is not mentioned in Scripture as having a wife, although it's possible he did have one.

But it would have been unusual for two women in the household, two sisters, to both have been unmarried beyond their mid-teens. No ages are given for anyone in the household. Our modern Sunday school eyes see these women as being in their late teens or early 20s—or maybe even a bit older.

They may well have been that old. And they may have been unmarried by choice, since their household appears to have been relatively wealthy. To have entertained Yeshua and his disciples as they did in Luke chapter 10, they would have had to feed upwards of 80 people! That's a lot of people to extend hospitality to, even if not every one of them was fed.

Another evidence of the wealth of this household was the fact that they had a family tomb. In John 11 we read the story of

36 Ascetics are people who dedicate themselves to contemplative ideals in prayer and to practices of sometimes extreme self-denial, usually for religious reasons. An ascetic leads an austerely simple life, particularly abstaining from the normal pleasures of life.

the raising of Lazarus, who dies from a serious illness. The gospel account of his raising makes it clear that the body of Lazarus is not buried in an ordinary grave dug into the ground, but in a tomb. Only the wealthy could afford tombs, something that is true today as well.

And then there is the perfume—ah, but let's wait until we get to that part of this Miriam's story. Suffice it to say that whether Miriam and Martha were widows who had not yet remarried, or whether they were wealthy girls who could afford not to marry, they are apparently without husbands in the Gospels.

Archeological Evidence of Lazarus, Martha and Miriam

Believers assume that the people named in the Gospels were real historical characters. For Lazarus, Martha, and Miriam, we may actually have archeological evidence of this. In 1873 an Arab sheik living on the eastern slopes of the Mount of Olives near the road to Bethany discovered a large cave beneath his house. A French archeologist named Professor Clermont-Ganneau was called in to investigate. The cave was a large burial chamber from the first century AD containing 30 limestone ossuaries, or bone boxes.

The burial custom in first-century Jerusalem was that rich people would either cut a family tomb into the rocks of the mountains surrounding the city or modify a small natural cave for that purpose. Several burial shelves would be hewn from the walls of the tomb. The dead would be covered in linen grave cloths, their chins tied shut with a linen napkin, their wrists and their ankles crossed and tied with linen also. Then a linen burial sheet would be wrapped lengthwise underneath the body, over the head and then covering the front of the body. Certain spices such as aloes and myrrh would be placed around the body to disguise the stench as it decayed in the hot climate.

The opening of the mouth of the tomb would be covered by a large stone shaped like a disk. The stone was quite heavy and served to seal the tomb and protect the body from marauding animals.

At a certain point, perhaps a year or more after the initial burial, the tomb would be opened. When all that was left of the body was bones, the bones would be placed in a special stone box, called an "ossuary," as a permanent burial. The box would be left in the tomb.

Some of the ossuaries in the tomb discovered in 1873 were inscribed with a cross or with the name "Yeshua" in Hebrew. On the sides of three of the ossuaries were inscribed the names, Lazarus, Miriam, and Martha in Hebrew. All three had the sign of the cross on them, indicating that they were Jewish believers in Yeshua. It is highly probable that the cave itself belonged to the family of Mary, Martha, and Lazarus mentioned in the Bible, according to Prof. Clermont-Ganneau.

Whether those ossuaries are connected with the same household in Bethany as the one mentioned in Scripture, we don't know for sure. But we do know that Lazarus, Martha, and Miriam were special friends of Yeshua, and they figure in some dramatic incidents in his life.

Let's look at three portraits of Miriam of Bethany.

Miriam, the Disciple

We first meet Miriam of Bethany in Luke chapter 10. Let me set this up for you. Yeshua has been traveling all over the countryside with his disciples, preaching and ministering to people, all the while training his disciples, who are learning by watching him and imitating what he says and does.

As they are traveling, they enter a village where a woman named Martha "welcomed Him into **her home**" (Luke 10:38). Although the passage in Luke does not identify the village as

Bethany, it does say that Martha had a sister named "Mary"—Miriam. Most scholars agree that this is the same Martha and "Mary" who are identified as living with their brother Lazarus in the Gospel of John. Therefore, this is a story about Miriam of Bethany and her sister, Martha.

The very fact that the home is identified as Martha's tells us that Martha is likely in charge of all household matters there and that Miriam is her younger sister. Translation: Martha is the boss, and Miriam is supposed to obey her directions.

On the day in question, Martha welcomes the famous itinerating Rabbi Yeshua into her home. In the Middle East even to this day, people are hospitable to travelers, even to strangers. Hospitality over the centuries has been a matter of life or death for many. But in Yeshua's case, to invite him to share a meal with you meant inviting his disciples also, because they are traveling with him.

Okay... that's like twelve more mouths to feed, right? Wrong. At this point in Yeshua's ministry, he was not only training the Twelve, but also a group known as the Seventy. In fact, the Seventy are featured in Luke's Gospel just a few verses before the story of Miriam and Martha. And in addition to the Seventy and the Twelve, Luke tells us at the beginning of chapter 8 that there were a group of women who also traveled with Yeshua. There were at least three of them, possibly more.

So when I total up all of this, I count at least 86 guests coming to dinner at Martha's house. Get the picture? Not an intimate little dinner party, but a big group of hungry travelers, plus hangers-on from the village, etc.

Now we probably all remember the story. Here it is in just a few verses in Luke:

> *Now as they were traveling along, He entered a village; and a woman named Martha welcomed*

> *Him into her home. She had a sister called* ***Mary, who was seated at the Lord's feet, listening to His word.*** *But Martha was distracted with all her preparations; and she came up to Him and said, "Lord, do You not care that my sister has left me to do all the serving alone? Then tell her to help me." But the Lord answered and said to her, "Martha, Martha, you are worried and bothered about so many things; but only one thing is necessary,* ***for Mary has chosen the good part,*** *which shall not be taken away from her."*[37] [emphasis added in bold

Our first encounter with Miriam of Bethany tells us she is a) Martha's sister and b) a person "sitting at the Lord's feet, listening to His word." From this very brief story we can sense that Martha is very likely the older sister, because she is clearly in charge of the house. And Martha is "distracted" (read: "stressed out to the max") with all her preparations. Eighty-six people for dinner? No problem, right?

Now to be fair, we know from several Gospel passages in John that Martha's household has some wealth. So, very likely (though the text doesn't say so) Martha had servants helping her. But she still needed her sister Miriam's help. This was definitely a time for "all hands on deck." So not surprisingly, Martha interrupts Yeshua as he is teaching, and probably with some exasperation and a sense of her own rights in the matter asks Yeshua to send Miriam back to the kitchen—or words to that that effect.

But Yeshua commends Miriam, while not being entirely unsympathetic to Martha. He says that Miriam "***has chosen the good part, which shall not be taken away from her.***"

37 Luke 10:38-42.

Miriam's Choice

What exactly has Miriam chosen? She has chosen to sit and listen, yes. But to see the significance of this, we need to understand both the customs of the day and a little Greek grammar. In that day a disciple of an itinerant teaching rabbi like Yeshua would be described as a person who was "sitting at the feet" of Rabbi So-and-so.

The Apostle Paul describes himself this way with respect to Rabbi Gamaliel in Acts 22:3. Certainly in a culture where chairs were a rarity, sitting on the floor or on the ground was the usual way one would listen to such a rabbi anyway. But this phrase "sitting at the feet" had an additional flavor to it, a sense that this rabbi was a person worthy of honor and devotion—at least in the eyes of the disciple, the person sitting at his feet.

The physical posture of sitting at the feet of a rabbi (who would likely be sitting on cushions or on a large boulder so he could be better seen and heard) was also a picture of the inner posture of the heart of the disciple. The idea was that the disciple savored every word and gesture from the rabbi because this man had acquired the art of living wisely and well before God and was a true master of both the Scriptures and the traditions interpreting them.

In the context of the disciple/rabbi relationship, the rabbi himself was the disciple's "textbook." It was the disciple's task at all times to observe closely everything he saw the rabbi do and everything he heard the rabbi say. All of this was so that the disciple could imitate the rabbi's actions and words to become, in his own words, "just like my rabbi."

Yeshua refers to this same concept in the Gospels in at least two places. In Luke 6:40 Yeshua says, "A disciple is not above his rabbi. But each one when he is fully trained **will be like his rabbi**." And in Matthew 10:24-25 he says something similar: "A disciple is not greater than his rabbi. It is enough for a disciple to **be like the rabbi**."

This is the goal of discipleship in Yeshua's time: to become like the rabbi. So now let's return to our Miriam. What is she doing at Yeshua's feet? Yes, she is sitting in the posture of a... **disciple**. Understand that in Yeshua's day, unmarried women were not welcomed as disciples of itinerant rabbis like Yeshua. The other women who traveled with Yeshua in those days were married or widowed women, with the possible exception of Miriam of Magdala.

I have seen artistic renditions of the scene at Martha's home, showing her sister Miriam alone in a room sitting at the Lord's feet and Martha coming into the room, arms crossed. But that's hardly likely. Instead, Miriam would have been sitting among many other disciples and onlookers who were also listening to the Master. More than likely they would have been sitting outside in the courtyard of the house.

The fact that Martha goes up to Yeshua and asks him to tell Miriam to get up and help her makes me think that maybe Martha is using Yeshua's rabbinic position as leverage in this situation. It also suggests that Miriam is sitting pretty close to his literal feet. I always picture her there, don't you? And indeed, the Greek verb used here in Luke 10:39, *parakathisasa*, literally means "to be seated beside." Likewise, the Greek verb translated "listening" adds to this sense of her being absorbed in his words. That word is *ekouen*, which carries with it the sense that her listening was a continuing or customary action of hers. A good paraphrase would be "who always used to listen to his teaching."[38]

Miriam is a "good girl," apparently unmarried. Unlike Miriam of Magdala, she is in no way able to travel with Yeshua

38 The Wycliffe Bible Commentary, Electronic Database, Moody Press. 1962.

and his other disciples because of her family ties and the cultural expectations for women in her social class and situation. Therefore, she has to make the most of every moment that Yeshua is in her house. Like every good disciple, she is sitting there studying him—his gestures, the look on his face as he speaks, his interactions with others around him, his manner of dress, his speech, and most of all, the teaching he gives.

In a sense she is gazing on his heart. She is drinking it all in, because he might not be there tomorrow or a few days from now, and she can't follow him to his next town or village. This is it—her only opportunity.

Remember back in chapter 1 we said there was an element of rebellion in the name "Miriam"? Well, this Miriam's rebellion may not seem like much to twenty-first-century minds, but within her culture, she stepped over several boundaries of gender and cultural conformity. One of them is this incident of her sitting at Yeshua's feet in the outward posture of the inward reality of her heart.

I don't believe that her motivation was rebellion. I'm just saying that to the outward eye of her contemporaries, her actions look like rebellion. It looked like she was rebelling against the cultural expectation that only men could be disciples of the rabbi. It looked like rebellion when she, a woman, sat beside Yeshua like one of his disciples, instead of back in the corner somewhere. It looked like she was rebelling against the cultural expectation that the women of the household should be focusing on food preparation, an extension of hospitality, rather than drinking from the well of life eternal Who was sitting in the courtyard.

Miriam, the Contemplative

Miriam of Bethany was actually counter-cultural in her time. And she models for us a counter-cultural type of lifestyle centered on a particular spiritual discipline that has been called "contemplative prayer" or "contemplation."

This ancient spiritual practice is a kind of contradiction in terms. We typically think of prayer as having some kind of words, whether we are speaking them aloud or only internally. But in contemplative prayer, the human participant is silent. Contemplation is a wordless prayer before God, in which God may or may not communicate anything more than His own silence in return. This is not the kind of prayer where we are asking God for anything. It's not intercession or supplication. It is not a declaration or confession. It is not repentance, or any other type of word-filled prayer.

It is simply a way to enter the presence of the Lord and just "be" with Him in silence. It is a way to enjoy Him without looking for anything in particular from Him. The idea is just to "gaze" on Him who is only visible to your heart, letting the experience of this change you.

How is Miriam an example of this? Well, in the text in Luke 10 we read that Miriam is just sitting and listening. She is just watching Yeshua, taking Him in along with His words. Notice that she is not conversing with him or asking him questions in this context. She is in total reception mode.

And what does Yeshua say about what Miriam is doing? He says that though the bustling Martha is flitting from task to task, **there is really only one thing that is necessary**. What is that one thing? Is it the Great Commission, "Go into all the world and preach the gospel"? Is it firing up the to-do list, even the spiritual to-do list or the church's to-do list, and going after it? Is it feeding the hungry, healing the sick, or tending His sheep? Or is it making priestly intercession for the people?

No. It is sitting at Yeshua's feet as a disciple and listening, listening habitually to his teaching. It is sitting still with a quiet heart, taking in his words and his very person. He says that experience will never be taken away from Miriam. It is **the one thing that is necessary**.

Miriam sat right at his feet and engaged with Yeshua, face to face. This kind of direct experience with Yeshua is quite foreign to many believers in our day, who have been told for years that studying the written Word of God, rather than actively pursuing direct contact with the Lord, is the way to develop a "relationship" with God. Indeed. many of us have been cautioned by well-meaning church leaders against "seeking after mystical experiences." By "mystical experiences" they meant having direct encounters, face to face, with Yeshua Himself, where He appears to the person or takes them into Heaven for an experience with Him, even beyond the immediate activity of Scripture study and meditation.

I want to make very clear that in no way do I intend to diminish the position of the written Word of God, the Bible, in the life of the believer. Actually, I would say that the better one knows the written Word of God, the greater that person's potential is for experiencing deep transformation through the kind of "prayer" or spiritual experience Miriam of Bethany represents.

But before we look at how one goes about practicing that kind of prayer, let's look a little further into Scripture to see if we can begin to understand why Yeshua said this activity was the one thing necessary.

Take a look at this. What Yeshua said about Miriam's action as being the "one thing necessary" builds on something David wrote in Psalm 27:

> ***One thing*** *I have asked from the LORD, that I shall seek: That I may dwell in the house of the LORD all the days of my life, To behold the beauty of the LORD, And* ***to meditate in His temple.*** (Verse 4) [emphasis added in bold]

David is saying, "All I want to do, Lord, is just be with You where You are, to drink in Your beauty—to gaze on You—and to ponder You and everything about life with You in Your temple."

Okay, I get it. David went into the Temple in Jerusalem and spent time in prayer.... But wait a minute. There wasn't a temple in David's time. That was built by his son Solomon in the next generation. I believe that David glimpsed something about the heavenly Temple and about the life in Heaven. It's a life where time is not an issue and where access to the Lord is also not an issue for those in Heaven with Him.

It's also a life where God—Father, Son and Holy Spirit—is revealed to us in His full glory. No wonder David was fascinated with the view!

Consider this also. In the Hebrew text the word that is translated "beauty" literally means "delightfulness." David is trying to find a word here that encompasses the delight that rises up in the heart of one who gazes on the Lord in His own house, in His own setting, where He is displaying the fullness of His glory.

Beholding His beauty leads one to meditate. Something about His Spirit's presence in this activity enters into our hearts and turns us to ponder Him and to ponder the issues of life in the context of knowing Him. In truth, the word in Psalm 27:4 which is translated "meditate" literally means "to inquire." It gives the sense of a conversation or an exchange between the one beholding the Lord and the Lord Himself. The inquiry here is along the lines of someone who is ignorant, coming to be filled with the experiential knowledge of God—experiencing God directly, rather than just hearing about Him from someone else. This is intimacy with God.

There's a transformational element here in this gazing. Beyond words, even the words from God which one might hear while gazing on Him, this kind of prayer changes us just by the doing of it. It changes one's **being**. What does it mean for us just to "be"? Be what? Be who? Without words, without visions or even tangible experience, sitting in the presence of God by faith changes us day by day, like water dripping on a stony heart which imperceptibly wears it away drop by drop.

After long practice of this type of prayer, our perception of distance from God has shrunk—as well it should, since He lives within us by His Spirit. Contemplative prayer is one of several paths on which the Lord may take us in order to bring us to a vital awareness of this aspect of eternal life: **God <u>with</u> us**. Christ in us, our hope of glory.[39]

Everlasting Life with God

Let's look at a key Scripture: John 3:16.[40] This verse is one of the basics. It tells us what God the Father had in mind when He sent His Son to live among us and then die on a cross. It gives us His heart motivation: love for the world. And it also tells us the kind of response He expects from us and what that response opens up for us: **everlasting life**.

Everlasting life could be defined in several ways, including the idea that our physical bodies are no longer subject to death. But in His prayer recorded in John 17:3, Yeshua defines "everlasting life" as ***"knowing the only true God and Jesus Christ whom He sent."*** If we look at the underlying Greek, we will find that the kind of "knowing" He is talking about here is a deep intimacy—not a superficial acquaintance.

According to this verse, what do we receive when we come to faith in Yeshua?

First, we shall not perish—that is, our eternal destiny will not be the Lake of Fire or Hell, however one defines that. And second, we shall have "everlasting life." We know from other

39 Colossians 1:27.
40 "For God so loved the world that He gave His only begotten Son, that whoever believes in Him should not perish but have everlasting life."

parts of Scripture that "everlasting life" is not simply "living forever." Every human soul will continue to exist after it departs this earth, though not all will go to live in the presence of God.

Part of the good news of the gospel message is that we can live this everlasting life right now, if we are in covenant with Yeshua. Right now, in this life on earth, we can know God intimately. Obviously, intimacy within any relationship is something that needs to develop over a period of time and through many circumstances.

How then do we develop intimacy with God?

Certainly, we can learn a lot about God from Scripture. I don't think Yeshua was implying in his response to Martha that the Scriptures are unnecessary or irrelevant to knowing God on a personal basis. He said on another occasion that not the smallest letter of the written Word of God would pass away until all of it was fulfilled (Matthew 5:18). That affirms the importance of Scripture.

Furthermore, Yeshua lived in a day where most Jewish people had memorized large portions of Scripture as children in the local synagogue schools. Even young girls typically memorized significant portions of Torah, as well as all the Psalms and Proverbs.

Consequently, maybe Yeshua assumed that anyone who was serious about pursuing God would already have a basic acquaintance with the core of the written Word of God. And much of Yeshua's teaching in the Gospels was actually an exposition or a revelation of what God already said about Himself through Scripture, primarily through the books of Deuteronomy and the Psalms and Proverbs.

But in addition to revealing Himself to us by His written Word, God also reveals Himself to us directly and personally by His Spirit. We know from verses such as I Corinthians 3:16 and II Timothy 1:14 that the Holy Spirit lives inside those who believe in Yeshua. Yeshua Himself said this about the indwelling presence of the Holy Spirit:

> *I will ask the Father, and He will give you* ***another Helper, that He may be with you forever; that is the Spirit of truth,*** *whom the world cannot receive, because it does not see Him or know Him, but you know Him because He abides with you and will be in you.* (John 14:16-17)

> *This is how Yeshua described the ministry of the Holy Spirit in our lives: I have many more things to say to you, but you cannot bear them now. But when He, the Spirit of truth, comes,* ***He will guide you into all the truth;*** *for He will not speak on His own initiative, but whatever He hears, He will speak; and He will disclose to you what is to come.* ***He will glorify Me, for He will take of Mine and will disclose it to you.*** *All things that the Father has are Mine; therefore I said that He takes of Mine and will disclose it to you.*
> (John 16:12-15) [emphasis added in bold]

Notice Yeshua said, "He will glorify Me, for He will take of Mine and will disclose it to you." The primary focus of the Holy Spirit in our lives today is to **reveal** Yeshua and the Father to us—to make them real to us, to bring us their words and help us experience the nature of their hearts.

In John 14:19 Yeshua tells His disciples that though the world will not see Him, **they (His disciples) will see Him.** Did you get that? His disciples will **see Him**. How and in what ways would they see Him?

We know from the text of the Gospels that they literally saw Him during the period of 40 days after the resurrection.

And we know from Scripture that He continued to appear in visions to people like Paul and like John on the island of Patmos even after His ascension to Heaven. If we say that we believe the Scriptures, then such experiences set a precedent for us who live in the time after the Scriptures were written.

Yeshua says further in John 14:21 (speaking of the time coming after His resurrection) that He will disclose Himself to **those who are obeying Him in love.** So it is not just to the Twelve or to the Seventy—or to the 500 people whom Paul refers to as having seen Yeshua post-resurrection (I Corinthians 15:6). He discloses Himself **to us now**, even in our day.

Now maybe you, like me, have heard of believers who have literally seen Jesus, in the same way that I am seeing these words on my computer screen as I am typing them. Maybe you are one of those believers yourself, or maybe you know someone who has had this experience, friends or acquaintances. I personally know two women who, in separate incidents, had their initial salvation experience when the Lord appeared to them right in their homes.

I also personally know several other people who have either seen Jesus walk into a room to perform an act of ministry or have actually spent time with Him in Heaven. All of the people I know who have had these kinds of experiences with the Lord give every appearance of complete sanity. None have any form of "epilepsy," which is the explanation some skeptics have given as a way to explain away these kinds of holy encounters.

I believe they *did* actually see the real Jesus, not a figment of their imaginations. I say that because in every case of this I have known, the life of the person having that experience made a huge change afterward. They did a "180," and suddenly everything shifted 180 degrees in the opposite direction, including their own personal agenda.

Yes, I believe that those experiences are real—and I sure

would love to have one myself. (Are you hearing me, Lord????!!) But that is not the picture that Miriam of Bethany presents for us. She is modeling a kind of "seeing" Jesus, seeing Yeshua, which depends as much on us as on Him.

Let me explain what I mean. Most of us have not seen Yeshua in the natural realm like Miriam did. But we have an advantage Miriam did not have. We have the Holy Spirit living in us. The Holy Spirit's focus right now is to make Yeshua real to us—to reveal things to us about his heart and character, for sure, but also to give us **spiritual encounters with Him**.

What do I mean by "spiritual encounters"? Well, of course having a supernatural experience with Yeshua in which He appears to your natural eyesight would constitute a spectacular spiritual encounter. But I am thinking more along the lines of the kind of experience people describe as "seeing Him in my heart" or "hearing Him in my spirit." Believe it or not, this kind of experience is actually part of the spiritual inheritance given to every believer in Christ. It is not reserved for the "super-saints" or the super-spiritual. But it does depend on some factors that are usually within the control of the believer. Pursuing this kind of heart-to-heart knowing is one of those spiritual disciplines that gets easier and deeper the more we practice it.

What is Contemplative Prayer?

I am going to lump all the possible techniques connected with what some would call "listening prayer," "prayer of the Presence," or "centering prayer" into one term: **contemplative prayer**. And yes, I know that what I am about to describe is not quite the classic four-part approach advocated in the writings of saints going back hundreds of years. For the sake of brevity (since this is not a book focused primarily on contemplative prayer) I am going to use Miriam of Bethany's approach as described in John as the simple model for experiencing this type of prayer.

In its simplest form, contemplative prayer is a kind of prayer where we just spend time with the Lord, without any agenda on our side—certainly no "prayer requests" as such—and often without any words at all.

Prayer without words? How can it be prayer if we don't ask God anything? Well, if you don't like this wordless activity being described as "prayer," then find another term. How about simply "being present with the Lord"? Here is a definition of this kind of prayer from Gary Wiens, who both practices this kind of prayer and teaches about it: "...enjoying intimacy with the Godhead in love, resulting in personal transformation." [41]I've also heard Gary and others such as Jim Goll and Joseph Garlington describe this kind of prayer (with a twinkle in their eye) as "just wasting time on Jesus."

Contemplative prayer is pictured in one of my favorite verses, II Corinthians 3:18. This verse says,

> *But we all, with unveiled face, **beholding as in a mirror the glory of the Lord,** are being transformed into the same image from glory to glory, just as from the Lord, the Spirit.* [emphasis added in bold]

As we look and see with the eyes of our heart the beautiful face of Yeshua, which was scarred for our deliverance—that face with eyes that connect us with the love that fills His heart—we are changed. Second Corinthians 3:18 says that we are changed into the same image! What this is saying is that if we spend time gazing at Him as a practice of life, we become more and more like Him.

Why? Well for one thing, there is something transforming, on a human level, about the activity of **gazing.** Gazing in this context is a *sustained watching or looking into another person's eyes.*

41 *Bridal Intercession: Authority in Prayer Through Intimacy with Jesus* (2001).

And gazing develops relationship. Even earthly psychologists recognize that a powerful bond is created between two human beings who gaze into each other's eyes. The bond between a mother and her newborn child is strengthened by her gazing into the baby's eyes. The bond between a man and a woman is often acknowledged and strengthened when they gaze into each other's eyes for even a few seconds.

On a human level, gazing develops intimacy. It's that simple. The more we gaze at someone, the greater the potential for deeper and deeper intimacy with that person, particularly if he returns the gaze. Increased intimacy transforms the quality of our lives, *because we were made for intimate relationship.*

Gazing into the eyes of another human being transforms us by increasing intimacy. The same thing is true with gazing upon God. But how do we gaze on someone who is invisible to us on earth? How do we, as a practical matter, look into His eyes?

The Lord told His disciples in John 16:12-14 that the Holy Spirit would remind them of what Yeshua had told them and would also give them things that Yeshua could not tell us while He was on the earth. Ephesians 1:17 speaks of this aspect of the Holy Spirit's ministry as "the spirit of wisdom and revelation in the knowledge of Him," referring to Yeshua and to the Father.

What that tells me is that the Holy Spirit will help me to understand the Father and the Son and will continuously reveal more to me about them. But He will also disclose what is Yeshua's and give it to us (John 16:12-14).

And the Lord Yeshua lives inside of us by His Spirit, if we are saved (II Corinthians 13:5). If that is so, then isn't it possible for me—and for you—to see Him with our hearts? Isn't it possible for us to gaze on Him, "in the Spirit" as it were?

Miriam of Bethany did not want merely to hear about what Yeshua said after He'd already said it. She didn't want to hear the reports of those who heard him firsthand. She wanted to *experience* him directly. She wanted to *experience* the force of His words and of His person—His heart, if you will. She wanted to partake of the Feast, not simply hearing what He said second hand—the spiritual "leftovers."

A Recipe for Encounter

Is this what you want too? Are you discontented hearing about the spiritual experiences others are having with the Lord, while you yourself don't feel as close to Him? Are you trying to live from the "leftovers" that someone shares with you from the pulpit, in a book, or on a Zoom call? Leftovers are wonderful if you also experienced the feast. Those leftovers help you relive that experience. But they can never replace the feast itself.

The Lord has made a way for every believer to be as close to Him as that believer wants.[42] Here, try this holy experiment. In the Book of Ephesians there are two prayers, one in the first chapter and the other in the third chapter.[43] Read those prayers and pick the one that resonates with your heart more.

Now for the next 21 days, personalize that prayer, praying it over your own life at least once a day. Do you know what I mean by that? Here's an example using the prayer in Ephesians 3 (my personal favorite):

> *Father, You from whom every family in heaven and on earth derives its name, please grant me, according to the riches of Your glory to be strengthened with power through Your Spirit in my inner being so that Christ, the Messiah, the Anointed One may dwell in my heart through faith, that I, being rooted and grounded in love may be able to comprehend with all the saints what is the breadth and length and*

42 See Rick Joyner's report of an encounter with the Lord where He told Rick this very thing. Page 140 of *The Final Quest*, MorningStar Publications, Charlotte, North Carolina, USA, 1996.
43 Ephesians 1:17-23 and Ephesians 3:14-20

> *height and depth and to know as a direct experience the love of Christ for me personally, which surpasses mere head knowledge about it, that I may be filled up to all the fullness of God.*[44]

Now this is not the only way or even the best way to phrase this prayer. I based it on the New American Standard translation for this passage, but then I modified parts of it to pull in ideas from the Amplified translation and from my own understanding of certain key words in the original Greek. You don't have to word the perfect prayer to get a good result, but you do need to engage your heart in what you are praying.

Using the same passage, here's how I might pray this more simply:

> *Abba, you are my Father. Please strengthen my inner being so that Yeshua may dwell in me by His Spirit through faith and I can experience His love for me directly and personally, getting a glimpse of the full dimensions of it, so that I may be filled up to all the fullness of God, even as my brothers and sisters before me were.*

You use your own words after you read that passage. Father is always looking at the intention of our hearts, rather than whether we use some special words or phrases.

Then each day after you pray your prayer, sit quietly in a chair in a room where you won't be disturbed. Set another chair across from you. That's the chair that will represent for you the presence of the Lord, the presence of Jesus. Now for about the next five minutes, think about His face. You can ask the Holy Spirit to reveal that face, if you want. What does His face look like today? What color are His eyes? What is His expression? Can you keep looking at Him? Does He say anything to you?

44 Based on verses 14-19.

What else are you experiencing?

OK. The first time you do this, you might not see or hear anything or feel anything special. And that might not even happen the tenth time you do this! This is not a formula for contemplative prayer or for having special spiritual experience with the Lord. This is more like an "on-ramp" that might put you on a highway that will take you to where *He* wants to take you.

Another Approach

But if that is not your cup of tea, try this one. Take out your bible (or your tablet or phone) and open it to any Gospel passage. Maybe you have a favorite one. Set that chair across from you and start reading the passage slowly aloud. Ask the Holy Spirit to bring the Lord's commentary to you, what He wants to say about that passage today. Then listen with your heart. Hear anything? If not, ask Him a question. How does He respond? With another question? Good. Now you are having a conversation with Rabbi Yeshua.

You're only going to spend a few minutes a day on this. And remember, this experiment continues for at least 21 days. If you're not seeing any change in your own heart about how you relate to Jesus or to the Gospels, my advice is, *don't give up*! Continue the experiment a little longer.

And if you *do* notice changes in yourself or in the way you are seeing Jesus in the Gospels, I know you will want to continue this prayer practice anyway. What you are experiencing is an ancient method of opening the door between you and the Lord a lot wider than it currently sits. Enjoy it, like Miriam of Bethany did.

Choose a Character

Another variation of this kind of experience can begin by your choosing one of the characters in the Gospel passage and watching the action from that person's viewpoint. Drink in the Lord's words. Treasure the expression on His face as He speaks to your heart. You could be one of the named characters in the passage or just a bystander.

Believe me, as strange as it may sound to us, opening yourself up to this kind of peaceful prayer without words is one of the greatest gifts you can give Yeshua in this life. If I give money to a ministry because I love Yeshua, I can usually go out and somehow obtain more money to replace what I gave away.

But the time I spend doing anything can never be replaced. That makes time one of the most valuable commodities we have as believers, and the Lord is very much aware of that. It's one thing to spend time on an activity that clearly advances the Kingdom of God in the earth. But it's a really special gift to Yeshua to spend time with Him personally where your chief delight is the pleasure of His company, even if it is silent.

What we are saying to Yeshua by our willingness to engage in a contemplative experience with Him is, "*It is worth it to spend this time in silence with You, not asking You for anything, even if You say nothing to me—even if I can't feel Your presence or see You with my heart. You are worth it.*"

In addition to being one of the most valuable gifts you could give the Lord, the practice of contemplative prayer is also one of the most transformative spiritual disciplines you could engage in over your lifetime on earth. Many of us find that to be true, even though at times it seems like nothing at all happened during the time of quiet.

Gaze on Him regularly, and let the experience transform you. Early in the practice of contemplative prayer you will come to realize that it is **the Lord who grants you** the prayer experience. The particular experience you have with Him each time is His gift to **you,** as every encounter He had with Miriam of Bethany was His gift to her.

Miriam, the Extravagant Worshipper

My second mini-portrait of Miriam of Bethany grows right out of the first one. Here is the text:

> *Jesus, therefore, six days before the Passover, came to Bethany where Lazarus was, whom Jesus had raised from the dead. So they made Him a supper there, and Martha was serving; but Lazarus was one of those reclining at the table with Him.* ***Mary then took a pound of very costly perfume of pure nard, and anointed the feet of Jesus and wiped His feet with her hair; and the house was filled with the fragrance of the perfume.*** *But Judas Iscariot, one of His disciples, who was intending to betray Him, said, "Why was this perfume not sold for three hundred denarii and given to poor people?" Now he said this, not because he was concerned about the poor, but because he was a thief, and as he had the money box, he used to pilfer what was put into it. Therefore Jesus said, "****Let her alone, so that she may keep it for the day of My burial.*** *For you always have the poor with you, but you do not always have Me."*[45] [emphasis added in bold]

I did say "the text," but in reality there are two additional accounts of this incident in the Gospels—one in Matthew 26

45 John 12:1-9.

and the other in Mark 14.[46] Both of these accounts in Mark and Matthew put the incident in Bethany, though neither one identifies the woman who anoints Jesus with her perfume. There is also one account of a woman anointing Yeshua with perfume in the Gospel of Luke, but it is not the same incident. (I will explain why later in this chapter.)

Let's clarify the picture. It is now less than a week before Passover, the critical Passover when Yeshua will be the Lamb that is sacrificed. It is clear from his comments here, and even more so in the accounts in Mark and Matthew, that Yeshua knows his death is at hand. What is not clear is whether Miriam of Bethany knows it. We are given no explicit motive for her actions in any of the Gospel narratives.

The incident takes place at a dinner honoring her brother Lazarus, who in the previous chapter in John was raised from the dead after having lain in his family's tomb for four days. And of course the dinner was also honoring Yeshua, who had raised Lazarus from the dead. In the verses that follow the passage I just quoted, John relates that a large crowd gathered near the site of this meal, not only to see Yeshua, but also to see Lazarus, whose fame as a man who came back from the dead was growing.

In fact, he was becoming so famous that the chief priest planned to kill him, because his testimony was causing so many in Judea to believe in Yeshua.

Now our text from John tells us that Martha was there serving (what else!). Therefore, you might think this dinner took place at Martha's home again. But John never identifies the location beyond "Bethany." However, Mark and Matthew both say that the dinner took place at the home of someone known as "Simon the Leper."

46 Both Matthew and Mark say that this supper happened "2 days before Passover," as opposed to the reference to 6 days in John. Note that John does not say the supper happened 6 days before Passover—just that Yeshua arrived there 6 days before Passover.

What an interesting name. Here's what I see in his name. This Simon is not someone who is currently suffering from leprosy. No, under Jewish law such a person had to live "outside the camp"—i.e., away from others without the disease, and cry "Unclean, unclean!" as he walked near healthy people so that they would know he was leprous (Leviticus 13:45).

In the Gospels Yeshua cleanses several lepers of their leprosy (Luke 17 and Mark 1, for example). I suspect strongly that Simon was also someone Yeshua had cleansed from leprosy. What do *you* think? I think that this man was called "Simon the Leper" because people in the early church knew him by this miracle. But that's just my personal opinion.

I want you to picture this. Yeshua and some of his disciples are sitting down to this supper. They would probably be sitting on the ground or maybe on cushions at best. Martha and her servants are serving the platters and bowls of food to the guests, who are likely talking about Lazarus having been raised back to life.

Then, in and among the women comes one particular woman. She has a stone box in her hand, made of translucent alabaster. Without saying a word she stands next to the seated Yeshua. Oblivious to all other activity in the room, she breaks open the white stone box. Fragrant oil infused with precious spikenard begins to flow from the box, all over Yeshua's head, all over his robe.

She drops to her knees in front of him and continues pouring the precious, fragrant oil over his bare feet. The room is now filled with the fragrance. All conversation has ceased, and every eye is on the woman as she removes the shawl that hides her hair and bows her head completely to the ground in front of his feet. She flips the long strands of her dark hair over her head, and in a motion that is at once worship and surrender, she begins to wipe his feet with her hair, spreading the spikenard all over his feet.

It's like a vignette—a private, framed moment between this woman and Yeshua—only it was *not* private. This act of worship is like saying, "I was wrong and You were right." It was like saying, "How could I ever honor You enough for what you did for my brother and my family?" It was like saying, "I surrender all that I am, all that I have to You. Nothing is too good for You. No worship is too extravagant, too costly or too humbling for me. You are worth it all. You are the best of the best—the Anointed One."

Jewish women in Yeshua's day (and Orthodox Jewish women of today) kept their hair covered, except in the intimacy of the family circle. To uncover one's head like this lacked social decorum, to say the least!

But why did Miriam of Bethany uncover her hair? She did it to wipe the feet of the man who had raised her brother from the dead. She used what the Apostle Paul described as a woman's "glory" (I Corinthians 11:15) as a mere rag to wipe the lowest and dirtiest part of this man's body, his feet.

This is an act of great humility, love, and worship. This is a picture of complete worship and surrender.

She is worshipping Him from her heart. She has taken the lowest position in the room, prostrating herself at His feet. And she has taken a jar of precious oil so costly that it was worth 11 months' wages for an average worker in that day, and just lavished it all over Him—"wasting it" on Him.

Then in a posture of total humility, she gets down on the floor, uncovers her hair, and uses it like a common towel on the part of His body that probably was the dirtiest at that moment. More than that—it was the part of the body that kings of that time used to signify their victory over the conquered when they put their foot on the neck or head of their enemy.

Miriam is not Yeshua's enemy. But a few days or weeks earlier when Yeshua had finally arrived in Bethany after her brother had died, she had said words to Him, words of accusation motivated by pain. All of us have said words like this to Him at one time or another. "Lord, why didn't You heal my brother?" "Lord, why do I have to live with this pain in my body?" "Lord, where is the money to pay these bills!"

"Why didn't You come through for me? Why am I suffering? Don't you care? I thought you loved me." We've all been there and more than once if we've known Him for any length of time.

But now Miriam is humbling herself in repentant surrender, in thanksgiving, yes, but something deeper than simple joy. Her act of worship is forever captured in this Gospel account, but it's not simply to honor her. It's also there as a model for us, an example of a heart of extravagant worship.

Think of the oil that is inside of YOU. You are like that alabaster jar. You have something so precious inside you that no one else ever had or ever will. You can pour out that inner life in you. You can pour it out and pour it out extravagantly, until it might seem to an observer that you are "wasting" it on Him today. You can "waste" your precious life on Him.

And you know something? It's never a waste. He's WORTH IT!

Yes, the world will say that you are wasting your life on Him—such a waste spending that time communing with Him, heart to heart. Some will say, "What you could have done with those hours you spent in His company! What you could have accomplished in this life!" But no—you did this instead. You did it for Him and with Him. You did it to please Him and to lose the possibility of living more independently from Him, because you love Him.

The beauty and intimacy of Miriam's act of worship is jarred by the critical words of at least one of the disciples. In this account Judas is singled out. In the other accounts this sentimentis echoed by at least a few of the other disciples on hand. Yeshua is swift to correct those pious-sounding criticisms of this act of pure worship and to defend Miriam's act. Clearly He was in no way offended or embarrassed by Miriam's unorthodox worship.

A Priestly Prophetic Act

At a deeper level Miriam's action that day was a prophetic act. What do I mean by this? What she did was to pour and smear fragrant oil all over the one who is called "the Christ," "the Messiah," a word which means "the anointed one" or "one smeared with oil."

In the Scriptures kings and priests were anointed with fragrant oil as a consecration to YHWH and a sign of His empowerment for their calling. We have the example of the prophet Samuel anointing first Saul,[47] then young David[48] to be king of Israel. David's son Solomon was anointed David's successor by Zadok the priest in the presence of Nathan the prophet.[49]

The prophet Elijah was instructed by Yahweh to anoint Hazael as king of Aram[50] and to anoint Jehu as king of Israel.[51] The turbulent reign of the usurper Queen Athaliah came to an end when seven-year-old Jehoash was anointed as king of Judah by Jehoida the priest.[52]

Priests and prophets were also anointed. In Exodus 30 Yahweh tells Moses to anoint Aaron and his sons as priests with fragrant oil, oil which was compounded by the perfumer's art.[53] Much later, Elijah is instructed to anoint Elisha as prophet in his place.[54]

---

47 I Samuel 10:1
48 I Samuel 16:13
49 I Kings 1:39
50 I Kings 19:15.
51 I Kings 19:16.
52 II Kings 11:12
53 Exodus 30:25
54 I Kings 19:16.

The reign of Yahweh's Anointed One (Messiah, Christ) is prophesied in several places in the Psalms.[55] Isaiah 61 describes the Anointed One as someone who would bring good news to the humble, bind up the brokenhearted, proclaim release to captives and freedom to prisoners.[56] Peter is privileged by God the Father to recognize that Yeshua is this prophesied Anointed One.[57] After Peter and John are released from arrest, a prayer in Acts 4 describes Yeshua as "Your holy servant Jesus, whom You anointed."[58]

When was Yeshua anointed? **The only references in Scripture to him being physically anointed with oil on earth are the incident with the penitent woman in Luke 7[59] and this incident with Miriam of Bethany**. (I am not saying that he did not receive other anointings from God the Father or in the realms of Heaven.)

Do you understand the deep significance of this? In both anointings, a person who was neither an ordained priest nor a prophet was tasked with anointing the most significant person in all of Scripture. On top of this, **both of these non-priests were women.** Two women are the only persons recorded in Scripture as physically anointing THE Anointed One! And He commends both of them for what they did.

Don't lose sight of this point. In a culture where only males were priests, this Miriam by her act of that moment is a forerunner of the priesthood of all believers, including women,[60] which is ushered in through Yeshua: the priesthood of the order of Melchizedek, of which Yeshua Himself is the High Priest.[61] There's such a depth here to ponder, to meditate about

55 Psalm 2:2, Psalm 137:17, for example.
56 Isaiah 61:1.
57 Matthew 16:16.
58 Acts 4:27.
59 The Luke 7 incident and the woman who anointed Yeshua with perfume and tears is not the same incident, nor the same woman as the incident involving Miriam of Bethany. I explain why later in this chapter.
60 I Peter 2:9.
61 Hebrews 3:1, Hebrews 5:6 & 10, Hebrews 6:20, Hebrews 7:17.

concerning what this woman did that day. She did more than break open a box of spikenard—**she broke open the way for all believers.**

Spikenard is a strong, intense fragrance. It probably stayed on Yeshua's hair and clothing for several days afterward. When he inhaled the remnants of that perfume, did he think about that woman's act of worship and surrender? It was actually only a few days later that he was arrested, tried, scourged and crucified. As he went through that ordeal, were there moments when that fragrance, still clinging to him, reminded him of this act of love, reminded him perhaps of the joy set before him, when multitudes would prostrate themselves before Him in worship and surrender?

And what of Miriam of Bethany? We don't know where she was on the day Yeshua died. She is not recorded as being at the scene of the crucifixion. But the fragrance of her worship clung to *her*, as well. How would she have felt, that she had so humbled herself before Him and those at the dinner? Glad she did it? Confused the day he died?

We don't pour literal spikenard on Him now when we worship Him deeply from the heart. I cannot say what it is that He experiences when we do this. In a sense worship is a two-way street. No, it's not that He worships us! But something tangible of His presence can come over us in great strength, like a cloud of spiritual fragrance, like someone responding and releasing His intense pleasure over us. That presence makes deep connection with our spirits. The power of that kind of experience leaves its own deposit in our spirits, like a lingering fragrance. It sweetens the day and sometimes the weeks going forward.

If we open ourselves up to repeat that experience by once again worshipping Him from the heart, that fragrance will once more come all over us. Is it that way for Him? I don't know for sure. But consider this: Part of the worship in the Temple consisted in burning incense, a fragrant cloud that ascended from a gold-clad altar in the Holy Place. I wonder if that incense of worship is a picture of what the Lord experiences from us when we worship Him now. After all, we *are* mobile temples of the Holy Spirit in the earth (I Corinthians 6:19).

Don't be Confused!

I mentioned earlier in this chapter that the incident recounted in John 12 is also mentioned in Mark and Matthew. Luke 7 also contains an account of an unidentified woman who does something similar:

> *Now one of the Pharisees was requesting Him to dine with him, and He entered the Pharisee's house and reclined at the table. And there was a woman in the city who was a sinner; and when she learned that He was reclining at the table in the Pharisee's house,* ***she brought an alabaster vial of perfume, and standing behind Him at His feet, weeping, she began to wet His feet with her tears, and kept wiping them with the hair of her head, and kissing His feet and anointing them with the perfume.*** *Now when the Pharisee who had invited Him saw this, he said to himself, "If this man were a prophet He would know who and what sort of person this woman is who is touching Him, that she is a sinner." And Jesus answered him, "Simon, I have something to say to you."*[62] [emphasis added in bold]

This is not the same incident as the anointing described in Mark 14, Matthew 26, and John 12. In this passage in Luke, the city where the dinner is taking place is not specifically

62 Luke 7: 36-40.

identified. However, of all the Gospel writers, Luke takes pains in methodically giving a chronological account of the events he is relating (Luke 1:1-4). The other three Gospels agree that the anointing they are reporting on took place during the week between what we call Palm Sunday and the day Yeshua was crucified. Luke, however, puts this incident in the middle of a string of ministry events that occur in Galilee closer to the beginning of Yeshua's itinerant ministry.

Understand the importance of this. Galilee is the northern part of Israel, different in geography and culture from Judea, where Bethany and Jerusalem are located. Remember I said that Bethany is a suburb of Jerusalem, located only about two miles from the old walls of the city.

It is curious that Simon is the name of the host of the dinner in Bethany and of the host of the dinner in Luke 7. But it is clearly *not* the same Simon. The Simon in the Bethany dinner holds the feast to honor Yeshua and Lazarus, whom Yeshua raised from death. And as we said, the Simon of the Bethany dinner is known as "Simon the Leper"—or maybe we would say, "Simon the Former Leper." He could not still have the disease and have all these people eating with him. The occasion is clearly one where Yeshua is honored by the other guests and by the woman who anoints him with her perfume.

But the Simon in Luke 7 actually treats Yeshua, his guest of honor, with disrespect. This Simon is described as a Pharisee. We could call him "Simon the Pharisee." Yeshua tells him at one point that Simon failed to show him the simple courtesy of giving him water for his feet or of kissing him in greeting. Simon the Pharisee is more interested in having Yeshua at his dinner as a curiosity for the possible entertainment of his guests, not to honor him.

And the woman who anoints Yeshua in Luke anoints him with her tears, as well as with perfume. The accounts of the anointing in the other 3 gospels do not mention weeping. What is more significant is that in Luke 7 Yeshua's defense of the woman focuses entirely on her act as a fruit of repentance. He makes no reference at all to her preparing his body for burial.

By contrast, in the incident in Bethany, Yeshua makes no reference at all to that anointing having any connection to repentance, though it may have had. And it is his disciples who raise the issues about the woman's act in Bethany. Whereas in Luke it is Simon the host who raises issues about the woman, especially as it relates to Yeshua's prophetic discernment.

In our Western culture we tend to think that a woman anointing Yeshua was a unique incident, something never seen before in the earth. Therefore, there could not have been two different women who coincidentally had the idea to pour perfumed oil on Yeshua's head. And it would follow, then, that the incident in Luke *had* to be the same one depicted in the other three Gospels, right?

But it turns out that pouring perfumed oil on a head of a liberator is a cultural practice still alive in modern times in the Middle East.

I remember seeing a picture on the front page of the *Chicago Tribune* during the first Gulf War, showing a Kuwaiti woman pouring perfume on an American GI as the US troops marched into Kuwait City to liberate it from the fleeing Iraqi army.[63]

Certainly Yeshua liberated Lazarus from an early grave, and in doing so He also liberated Miriam, who probably would have faced an uncertain economic future without her brother. And certainly Yeshua liberated the unnamed women in Luke 7 from a life of shame and failure.

I believe that there was a large measure of repentance in the hearts of both women demonstrated in their extravagant acts

63 https://www.gettyimages.com/detail/news-photo/kuwaiti-woman-offers-rose-water-to-a-us-soldier-as-a-sign-news-photo/465359762?adppopup=true

of worship. But I will explain what I mean by that in a later chapter.

One more tangled knot of tradition I'd like to untangle has to do with misidentifying Miriam of Bethany as Miriam of Magdala. In the early post-Constantine centuries of the Catholic Church, Pope Gregory I confused these two Miriams, possibly because he did not have access to all of the New Testament scriptures. At Easter in 591 AD he preached that Miriam of Magdala was the woman who anointed Yeshua before the crucifixion. Nowhere in any Gospel account is she identified as ever having anointed Yeshua. Oops!

Unfortunately, Pope Gregory's error was then picked up and magnified by others during the medieval period. Even today you can find contemporary Christian writers who mix up the stories of these two Miriams because they have not carefully observed the details of these Gospel accounts, instead relying on classic commentaries that were…wrong. It makes such a dramatic, redemptive story: A demonized woman caught in sin encounters Yeshua's ministry and repents. She is delivered of seven demons and is then welcomed back into her family in Bethany—even though in the Gospels she is always identified as coming from Magdala!

Yes, that narrative of the "prodigal daughter" is dramatic—but those details are not supported by the scriptural narratives we have just examined. Now that you know that, don't be confused by those well-meaning writers and preachers. Miriam of Bethany and Miriam of Magdala are two very different persons.

Questions for reflection, discussion and journaling…

1. *If sitting at Yeshua's feet is the "one thing that is necessary," how do you do that in the 21st century?*

2. *Have you engaged in any prayer practice that consisted in just sitting wordlessly, engaging the very presence of God? What happened when you did this? Did your heart hear Him saying anything to you?*

3. *If you engaged in that type of prayer over a period of time, did it change you in any way? How would you describe the change?*

4. *Take a look again at Psalm 27, verse 4. Does any of the sentiment expressed in that verse resonate with you? If so, what specifically?*

5. *If we consider Yeshua's definition of everlasting life as "knowing the only true God and Jesus Christ whom He sent," how intimately are you currently living in this concept? If you are going to live forever, how closely do you want to live with the Lord in that forever?*

6. *Do you have a friend or relative who has actually seen Yeshua (Jesus) in this physical realm or in Heaven? What did you think of that when you heard them tell about it?*

7. *Can you identify with Miriam of Bethany's pain after her brother's death, when she says to Yeshua, weeping, "Lord, if you had been here, my brother would not have died"? What happened in your situation that caused you to question His actions, His purpose or His timing? Do you still carry a hurt there that needs healing?*

8. *Have you ever experienced a moment of worship where you slipped to your knees or prostrated yourself on the floor because you were overwhelmed by the glorious presence of God or perhaps overcome by extreme gratitude for something He did? What were your feelings?*

V

THREE MORE MIRIAMS!

Scripture Preview:
John 19:25-26
Romans 16:6
Acts 12:11-12

So far we have found four Miriams in the Bible. But there are at least three more.

These three Miriams have far less written about them in Scripture. That does not mean they are unimportant people. Indeed, I would argue that the fact that they are mentioned in Scripture means that they were well-known to members of the early church.

Of these three remaining Miriams, the one who has the most written about her in Scripture is Miriam, the mother of James and Joseph (or "Joses"). She is also referred to as "Mary of Clopas." This title in Greek could have been describing her as the "daughter of Clopas" or as the "wife of Clopas." Let's take a look at several references to her in the Gospels.

Miriam of Clopas

Actually, this Miriam is mentioned in all four Gospels in connection with the crucifixion and burial of Yeshua. Remember we discovered that John was the only male disciple of Yeshua who stood near the cross during the crucifixion? And remember we saw that Miriam of Nazareth (Yeshua's mother) and Miriam of Magdala were also standing there? Well, there was a third Miriam standing there also—Miriam of Clopas:

> *But standing by the cross of Jesus were His mother, and* ***His mother's sister, Mary the wife of Clopas,*** *and Mary Magdalene. When Jesus then saw His mother, and the disciple whom He loved standing nearby, He said to His mother, "Woman, behold, your son!"*[64] [emphasis added in bold]

The words "the wife" were supplied by the translator. They do not appear in the Greek text. And did you notice something else about this Miriam? She is identified as "His mother's sister." Now it would be unusual to say the least (though not unheard of in human history!) for two sisters in the same family to have the same name. Thus it is not likely that this Miriam was literally the blood sister of Miriam of Nazareth. But she could well have been her sister-in-law.[65]

Miriam, the Helper

Whether Miriam of Clopas was a sister or a sister-in-law of Miriam of Nazareth, she was **Yeshua's aunt**. In Matthew 27:55, which is a description of the women who were present at the crucifixion, her name is mentioned in a list of women who had followed Him from Galilee "while ministering to Him."

64 John 19:25-26.
65 If you want a closer look at possible alternative interpretations for this relationship, see the Wikipedia article on "Mary of Clopas."

Therefore, this Miriam was apparently from the Galilee region (which makes sense if she was related to Miriam of Nazareth), and she was attached to Yeshua's ministry as someone who traveled with his group and "ministered" to him.

What does that mean, "ministered to Him"? The underlying Greek is the same word we get our word "deacon" from. A deacon is someone who serves in the church. It could even be someone who literally serves food, as in Acts 6:2, where the apostles appointed deacons to wait tables.

Thus it sounds like this Miriam did some of the cooking and cleaning for Yeshua's traveling group. Who would she be in today's church? She would be a person who makes the coffee, prepares the elements of communion, babysits the kids while their parents met together, makes sure the preacher has his bottle of water on the podium, etc.

In other words, this Miriam is a picture of the **ministry of helps**. "Helps"? Is that scriptural? It sure is—and it's a spiritual and even supernatural ministry. Here is the scriptural reference:

> ***And God has appointed in the church,*** *first apostles, second prophets, third teachers, then miracles, then gifts of healings,* ***helps,*** *administrations, various kinds of tongues.*[66]

Helps—the God-appointed workers that make the church run. Take a look at your hand. Now consider each finger on that hand representing one of the five God-appointed ministries mentioned in the forth chapter of Ephesians: apostle, prophet, evangelist, pastor and teacher. Sometimes these are referred to as the "five-fold ministry gifts."[67]

OK. Now look at that hand closely. Without that area of your hand called the palm, none of those fingers can do their

66 I Corinthians 12:28
67 Apostle, prophet, evangelist, pastor, teacher.

thing. None of them are supported without the palm—none of them would be able to move, right?

Well, that palm is the ministry of helps. That palm is the greeters, the ushers, the parking lot attendants, the sound system person, the video editor, the church secretary… Are you getting the picture?

But I said helps is a "supernatural" ministry. Where does the supernatural come in to it? It comes by the anointing of the Holy Spirit and by doing whatever you do to the glory of God (I Corinthians 10:31). It comes from the fact that it says in the beginning of I Corinthians 12:28 (mentioned above) that "**GOD** set into the church…" GOD did it—therefore it is supernatural, and as a result, supernatural empowerment is available as a flow to anyone who engages in the ministry of helps.

Here is a quote from Buddy Bell, probably the foremost expert in recent decades on the significance of the ministry of helps in the running of a church. Brother Bell (as he likes to call himself) has trained thousands of ushers and greeters in particular and has inspired thousands of others to understand the ministry of helps as a holy and supernatural ministry.

Here is one of Brother Bell's favorite descriptions of the ministry of helps, which he says comes from W. B. Godbey, a nineteenth century Wesleyan holiness minister:

> *"O-O-O-O-O-Oh! The infinite value of the humble gospel helpers.* Thousands of people having no gifts as leaders are #1 helpers. How grand revival work moves along when red-hot platoons of fire-baptized helpers crowd around God's heroic leaders of the embattled host!"

Brother Bell finishes the quote by remarking, "***What a definition for a dirty-diaper changer!***"[68]

Absolutely. Think about it. What if that person making coffee or preparing the communion elements is praying in the spirit, declaring blessings over the work of her hands that morning? How about that dirty-diaper changer, telling that little baby how wonderful he is, how he is a mighty man of valor who will sit as a king in the heavenly realms? Or what about the greeter at the door who makes it a point to shake hands and look at folks right in the eyes as they come through the door?

Even that greeter's touch ministers peace and love into troubled or lonely hearts. Maybe that is the only time that week that some will be touched by another human being.

And the usher who responds to the nudge of the Holy Spirit to seat this couple near the front in the honored guest section, where they have never sat before in any church meeting—what about *him*? Supernatural power flows through all these ministries.

In fact I would say that serving in a helps ministry is a good way for us ordinary believers to start flowing in the power of the Holy Spirit, who loves to help people. Here are several notable examples from Scripture. First, here is the Lord's description of a man named Bezalel:

> *I have filled him with the Spirit of God in wisdom, in understanding, in* ***knowledge, and in all kinds of craftsmanship,*** *to make artistic designs for work in gold, in silver, and in bronze, and in the cutting of stones or settings, and in the carving of wood, that he may work in all kinds of craftsmanship. And behold, I Myself have appointed with him*

68 To get the full impact of this definition, you need to hear Brother Bell tell it. Go to You Tube and search for "Dr. Buddy Bell favorite definitions for the Ministry of Helps." Here is the address for this clip: www.youtube.com/watch?v=uknwDupTsg0. The clip is less than 5 minutes in length, but so worth watching and listening to.

> *Oholiab, the son of Ahisamach, of the tribe of Dan; and in the hearts of all who are skillful I have put skill, that they may make all that I have commanded you.*[69] [emphasis added in bold]

Notice that the Lord says **He** has filled Bezalel with His own Spirit, filling this man with wisdom, understanding, knowledge and a wide variety of "craftsmanship." This is a man who understands how to work with precious metals, with bronze and with wood. He understands the craft of cutting precious stones and how to set them. Another man, Oholiab, is appointed to co-labor with Bezalel.

Then God says something that applies to all of us. He says, "***In the hearts of all who are skillful I have put skill.***" What does that mean for us? It means, whatever we are skilled at, the talent for that thing was given to us by God. What are you good at? What do you enjoy doing? Whether it is a physical skill or ability like metalworking or long-distance running, or something more social like the ability to encourage others or comfort troubled souls, that talent was given to you by God. It was given to you so that you could do what He needs you to get done.

Your talent might be useful in an obvious ministry setting. But it might be that your talent or ability is either something that God has put in you to bless those around you or just to bless Him! The key is to find out what you like doing, what you're good at doing, and ask Him what He wants you to do with that ability. You might be surprised by the doors it opens for you.

So Miriam of Clopas is a "minister of helps." Now I did quote you several verses here, including the eyewitness account of John, who put Miriam of Clopas at the foot of Yeshua's cross. Why is she there? Because she loves him. Because he is in agony,

---

69 Exodus 31:3-6.

dying—in need. But this time the only help this Miriam can offer him is her presence.

However, perhaps this Miriam offered the others standing at the foot of the cross more tangible help. Perhaps Yeshua's mother leaned on this Miriam's presence for emotional support or physical assistance. Perhaps Miriam of Magdala and young John the disciple also looked to this older and wiser Miriam for help.

The scripture account doesn't say. But to get a better sense of her heart, let's look where else the ministry of helps probably took Miriam of Clopas. A few days later, after the double Sabbath of Passover and the weekly Sabbath, this happens:

> *When the Sabbath was over, Mary Magdalene, and Mary the mother of James, and Salome,* ***bought spices, so that they might come and anoint Him.*** *Very early on the first day of the week, they came to the tomb when the sun had risen. They were saying to one another, "Who will roll away the stone for us from the entrance of the tomb?" Looking up, they saw that the stone had been rolled away, although it was extremely large. Entering the tomb, they saw a young man sitting at the right, wearing a white robe; and they were amazed. And he said to them, "Do not be amazed; you are looking for Jesus the Nazarene, who has been crucified. He has risen; He is not here; behold, here is the place where they laid Him. But go, tell His disciples and Peter, 'He is going ahead of you to Galilee; there you will see Him, just as He told you.'" They went out and fled from the tomb, for trembling and astonishment had gripped them; and they said nothing to anyone, for they were afraid.*[70] [emphasis added in bold]

70 Mark 16:1-8.

Some scholars believe that Miriam of Clopas was also the Mary referred to as "the mother of James and Joses" and as "the mother of James" in other Gospel accounts. They come to this conclusion by harmonizing certain details about the crucifixion and resurrection accounts in the four Gospels. For purposes of this book, I am going to agree with these scholars and assume that Miriam of Clopas is the Mary identified in this passage from Mark 16 as the mother of James and Joses.

What was she doing at the tomb? Matthew says these women came to "look at the grave." But Mark has a little more information about it. He says they "bought spices." They took the time to stop off at a vendor on the way and buy what they thought they would need to finish the burial that took place so hastily a few days earlier.

Mark also says that those spices were going to be used by the women to "anoint Him." How ironic! Remember how Yeshua said of Miriam of Bethany that her act of pouring fragrant oil over him was to anoint him for death? And now another Miriam is going to anoint him after death—or so she thinks, because He who was entombed is the Anointed One, the Christ, who is no longer in the grave.

Miriam of Clopas does not complete the task she came to perform. Instead, she and the other women have the encounter with the angel at the tomb. Notice she is just doing her ministry of helps, just showing up with the others to minister to the needs of one who is beyond help or maybe "helpless." She is thinking that her dead nephew can't help himself at that moment. But because of her faithfulness to be who she is and therefore do what she does, Miriam of Clopas becomes an eyewitness to the evidence of the greatest event in human history: the resurrection of Yeshua.

Notice her response. She runs off with another woman (we know that Miriam of Magdala stayed and encountered the risen

Lord), and they are so afraid, they say *nothing*. Well, that's what Mark reports. Maybe they said nothing along the way as they went. But Luke says that in addition to the three women at the tomb whom Mark reported, there were also other women at the tomb and that all of them "*were telling these things to the apostles. But these words appeared to them as nonsense, and* ***they would not believe them***" (Luke 24:11).

Notice this: Miriam of Clopas became one of the first witnesses to the resurrection of Yeshua, all because **she showed up to help**. Who knows what *you* will see when you show up to help?

Miriam, the Hard Worker

Another one of the Miriams in Scripture is simply described by her activity in Romans 16:6:

> *Greet Mary, who has* ***worked hard*** *for you.*

This Miriam's name occurs in a list of people the Apostle Paul wants particularly to remember. The list includes, for example, Priscilla and Aquila, the tentmakers whom Paul met in Corinth. These two risked their lives for Paul, according to the text of this letter. And the list of greetings include one to Epaenetus, whom Paul describes as "the first convert to Christ from Asia" (modern Turkey). Then there are greetings to Adronicus and Junias, kinsmen and Paul's fellow prisoners, whom he describes as "outstanding among the apostles."

That is high praise. But the greeting to Miriam the Hard Worker falls right in between Epaenetus and those outstanding apostles. That might be sheer coincidence, but I think not. As you read down the list in Romans 16, a lot of folks are just listed by name. But Miriam is described as one who "has worked hard" for the fledgling church of Rome.

What catches God's attention? Ever wonder about that? In one sense nothing escapes His notice. But here in this chapter we see the name of a woman apparently not mentioned anywhere else in Scripture who is identified only as a hard worker. We know that works alone do not impress God. But faith expressing itself in works? Love manifested as works? That is what I believe gets the attention of God—enough to get a woman named Miriam a mention in the Word of God. Everyone who reads Paul's letter will read about her. Forever.

Miriam, Mother of John Mark

One more Miriam who is only mentioned once in scripture is found in Acts 12. Let's begin at the beginning of this story:

> *Now about that time Herod the king laid hands on some who belonged to the church in order to mistreat them. And he had James the brother of John put to death with a sword. When he saw that it pleased the Jews,* ***he proceeded to arrest Peter also.*** *Now it was during the days of Unleavened Bread. When he had seized him, he put him in prison, delivering him to four squads of soldiers to guard him, intending after the Passover to bring him out before the people. So Peter was kept in the prison, but* ***prayer for him was being made fervently by the church to God.*** [emphasis added in bold]

Herod has imprisoned Peter during the Passover. (Hmm, just like Yeshua was.) It's interesting that 16 soldiers (four squads of four) were assigned to guard this one man. Maybe Herod remembered how the body of Yeshua disappeared years earlier. The "ATS Bible Dictionary" says that Herod had adopted the Roman custom of having two soldiers in prison with the prisoner and two guarding the prison door.[71] Every three hours they would be relieved by another squad.

Peter must have been considered a very important prisoner. But:

> *On the very night when Herod was about to bring him forward, Peter was sleeping between two soldiers, bound with two chains, and guards in front of the door were watching over the prison. And behold,* ***an angel of the Lord suddenly appeared*** *and a light shone in the cell;* ***and he struck Peter's side and woke him up****, saying, "Get up quickly." And his chains fell off his hands. And the angel said to him, "Gird yourself and put on your sandals." And he did so. And he said to him, "Wrap your cloak around you and follow me." And he went out and continued to follow, and he did not know that what was being done by the angel was real, but thought he was seeing a vision. When they had passed the first and second guard,* ***they came to the iron gate that leads into the city, which opened for them by itself; and they went out*** *and went along one street, and immediately the angel departed from him.*[72] [emphasis added in bold]

Wow, really bizarre, right? Put yourself in this story for a moment. Pretend you are Peter, awakened from a sound sleep—and *that* by the way is also remarkable. Remember, Peter was the disciple who was so scared of being arrested with Yeshua that he denied knowing him. But here in the book of Acts, he is cool as a cucumber, sleeping the night before his anticipated execution.

71 online at biblehub.com: a "quaternion of soldiers."
72 Acts 12:6-10.

OK, you wake up because an ANGEL is hitting you in the side—maybe with a staff. Then the angel instructs you to get your shoes and coat on and follow him. Wouldn't you wonder if you were just dreaming of this jailbreak? Yeah, me too. And then there's that iron gate on the prison that just swings open by itself! Freaky, right?

Suddenly the angel disappears. Where do you go? What do you do? I know what you do—go to the house of someone in Jerusalem you trust, someone who is a believer, someone known for hospitality, who will take you in until you can get your bearings. I've got it: Miriam, John Mark's mother.

> *When Peter came to himself….**he went to the house of Mary,** the mother of John who was also called Mark, **where many were gathered together and were praying.***[73] [emphasis added in bold]

John Mark was one of Yeshua's disciples or at least a hanger-on. He was not one of the Twelve but may have been one of the Seventy.[74] Several years after Yeshua's resurrection, John Mark becomes a missionary companion to Paul for a while, although he seems not quite ready for it (Acts 15:37-39).

But the event in Acts 12 is the only reference to John Mark's mother. Notice that the place is described as the "house of Mary." And if you read the passage further down, you find that the house was big enough to have a gate and a servant girl named Rhoda. No wonder it was a gathering place for the believers who were praying for Peter.

This Miriam was a woman of means, a believer who opened her house for prayer in a desperate situation. I'm not at all sure from the text whether Peter knew that the prayer meeting was

73 Acts 12:11-12

74 See Luke 10:1 & 17 for mention of a group of 70 disciples of Yeshua who were being trained in ministry.

going on there. But he did know that this woman, this Miriam would be sure to get a message to the leaders of the church, letting them know of his miraculous escape. He did tell the people gathered in Miriam's house his story about the angel springing him from jail, and then he left to spend the night elsewhere (Acts 12:17).

Just consider how important this Miriam is. Her ministry might well have been more than we know of from this brief mention. But at a minimum, we know that she used what she had to do what she could. The saints gathered for prayer at *her* house. And she was so well-known to the company of believers that Peter went there first.

I know the text does not say this, but I'd be surprised to find out that she sent Peter on his way that night empty-handed! She probably had the servants quickly assemble some food and clothing and likely some money as well for Peter's journey. The text does not say where he went, but he probably left Jerusalem quickly and clandestinely.

What an adventure! What a *supernatural* adventure, and Miriam was in the middle of it.

Notice that all three of the Miriams in this chapter were just ordinary people who were doing what they always did—and found themselves remembered in the written Word of God. What honor.

Did you know that what you and I do here on earth is chronicled in Heaven? What we do is written in Heaven's books (Revelation 2:12 and other scriptures). What would you like to see written about you? *"She stayed at her post and served the Lord well, doing..."? "She worked hard, caring for the sick, encouraging the dying, praying for the release of prisoners, giving into clandestine missions work in dangerous places..."?*

What was it the Lord said? "***He who is faithful in a very little thing is faithful also in much.***" (Luke 16:10) If we are faithful in what the Lord gives us to do here in this life, even if it seems to us like it's something the size of a dot, the Lord will give us more responsibility, more to be faithful over—now, and in eternity. That was the principle illustrated by the Parable of the Talents in Luke 19, right?

Questions for reflection, discussion and journaling...

1. *Did you know about the ministry of helps before you read this chapter? This ministry is not limited to things done in connection with church. Helps is a ministry we all have all the time. Can you think of 4 or 5 things you've done in the last 24 hours to help or support someone else?*

2. *If someone like the Apostle Paul was mentioning you in his letter, what would you hope he would say about you? What aspect of your life would you hope grabbed his attention?*

3. *Has anyone ever told you that you have a gift for hospitality? Are you the relative whose house is the gathering place for family celebrations? Do out-of-town friends and relatives love to stop by your place on their way through? Don't make light of this wonderful, much appreciated gift!*

4. *Are you a giver, a generous soul? Would you have been the one to pass the hat the night Peter showed up at Miriam's house so that he had some provision for his immediate journey? Or maybe you would be the one who would leave the prayer meeting with him so that you could shelter him for the night in your own home?*

VI

THE EIGHTH MIRIAM

Scripture Preview:
I Corinthians 12:27

We have one more Miriam to consider. She is described in this passage from Mark 15:

> *There were also some women looking on from a distance, among whom were Mary Magdalene, and Mary the mother of James the Less and Joses, and Salome. When He was in Galilee, they used to follow Him and minister to Him; and there were* ***many other women who came up with Him*** *to Jerusalem.* (v.40-41) [emphasis added in bold]

"Many other women" with Him—who are they? Just some "Miriams"....just some women (whether they were named Miriam or not) who followed Yeshua and His disciples from the countryside and went up with them to the great feast of Passover.

I did quote this scripture for a reason, but not to talk about those women. I want to talk about the Miriams reading this book, whether or not their given name is "Miriam." You see, the written Word of God is meant to be a kind of mirror, that when we look into it we can see ourselves as God sees us. And what I'm seeing after looking at all the portraits of the Miriams in Scripture is that you and I are no different than these women. Yes, we live in a different time and place, but these women were just like us.

Can you find yourself pictured among any of these women? No? Oh, I get it—they were so good, so saintly and perfect in their ways that it's no wonder God called them to work for His Kingdom. Is that what you think?

Well, I don't blame you. I neglected to tell you a few more things about these Miriams.

Miriam of Exodus teamed up with her brother Aaron to lead a rebellion against God's chosen leader—her other brother Moses (Numbers 12:1 and following).

Miriam of Nazareth, highly revered by believers through the centuries, apparently thought her son was "*meshuggah*"—nuts—and brought his brothers along with her in an attempt to get him to abandon his ministry and come home with her (Mark 3:31-32).

Miriam of Magdala jumped to the conclusion that someone had stolen the body of her dead Messiah, rather than remembering what He had said about rising from the dead (John 20:2).

Miriam of Bethany was so deeply hurt by Messiah's failure to come in time to heal her dead brother Lazarus that she threw it in His face when He did arrive: "*Lord, if You had been here, my brother would not have died!*" (John 11:32).

Doubtless the other Miriams in Scripture also failed to live lives of perfect faith before Him—***just like all of us***. And that is just the point. They are just like us; we are just like them. So I am going to challenge you now. I have prepared a kind of holy experiment for you. I have chosen one of the mini portraits from each of four Miriams we have looked at, and I have written a little story about them, but I have moved that story into the twenty-first century. Each Miriam is doing the ministry we saw her doing in the Word of God. But I have set her story in modern times.

Each one begins with the statement "**I am Miriam**." I want you to read each of these aloud. I will give you more instructions after you finish.

I

The Watcher

I am Miriam. I live in the poorest neighborhood of this busy city. My mother works hard to keep my brothers and me fed and clothed. One day she left my baby brother with me, told me to watch him because the daycare couldn't take him for some reason. I don't know why. I was only nine years old. But hey, you grow up fast in my neighborhood.

That day it was nice outside. So me being me, I took the umbrella stroller down from the peg where it was hanging, opened it wide, and put my six-month old brother in it, like I saw my mother do. I rolled him down the city block to the park. I thought he would like all that green and the blue sky and all.

But all of a sudden, a car came screaming around the corner, and I heard the shots. I grabbed my little brother out of that stroller and rolled on the grass with him. He started to wail like crazy, but I did not lift my head until

I heard the sirens coming. We were not hurt, but a couple of kids who were over on the swings were shot pretty bad. I started to cry.

One of the ladies who lived down the street from us ran out to see what was going on. I was just lying on the ground, still afraid to get up. She yelled to me, "MIRIAM! Are you all right, child? Where is your mama?"

A cop came over to me. He was such a big guy that I was afraid of him too. But he had a quiet voice, at least with me. He stooped over and asked me if I was OK or was I hurt anywhere. I said, "No, I'm fine."

And he said, "What about the baby?"

"Oh, he's fine too. I didn't squash him any."

That's when the cop looked into my eyes and said, "Young lady, you saved this baby's life today. Does he belong to you?"

"No, sir!" I answered stoutly, "He's my brother!"

The cop laughed softly and said, "Where do you live? We'll take you home now." And then a lady cop came. She picked up the baby and began rocking him while she said something real quiet to him. He just stopped crying and kept looking at her face, like it was the most interesting thing he'd ever seen.

The lady cop said to me, "What's your name, honey?" "Miriam," I answered.

"Well, Miriam, how 'bout we take you and your brother home? Could you push the stroller for me?" And that's

how we got back home. She called my mom on her police phone when we got there. She told Mom she'd stay with me until Mom got back.

What a day.

II

The Intimate Intercessor

I am Miriam. It's a long time now since I did not have any relationship with Him. I have known Him for so many years that I can only vaguely remember what it felt like not to know Him. My days are filled with conversations with Him. Sometimes I speak out loud—I really like to do that when no one else is listening. It makes our conversation seem more real, less "imaginary," as some people would like to put it.

I tell you, there's nothing "imaginary" about Him! Before I got to know Him, I NEVER could have imagined He would be like that—so approachable, so caring, so down to earth, if you know what I mean—so much love in His eyes. Yet so wise beyond anyone I have ever known, so strong in His connection to me, and so powerful. He never pushes me away, never says He doesn't have time for me. Me on the other hand.... Well.

I read His letters to me every day. There are so many of them, and they are so rich, so full of wisdom, power, and life. The thing about them is, they seem to be alive, in an odd sort of way. Like they are always relevant to my life, no matter what they're addressing at that moment. It's like His letters have eternity written into them.

But what I treasure most is our history together. We've been through so much together, He and I. Yes, we've been through lots of storms and battles—and ***most*** *of them were against our common enemy. Still, I have to admit that I* ***have*** *wrestled with Him, wrestled even against His acceptance of me, against His loving me. But I've never won. Not once. He always wins, and I know He always will. Why can't I remember that when the thought comes to me to wrestle Him again?*

But you know, it's even those wrestling matches that have shown me the character and nature of His heart, the core of His being. I can't get away with ANYTHING. Nothing is hidden from Him. But that in itself is so freeing—I can't tell you! Not to have "fig leafs and aprons" on, trying to hide my nakedness, when all along He has covered me with His own robe. It's so great just to be "real" with Him. No pretense, you know?

All of this, my friend, has built something like a house of intimacy around Him and me. I know that I can ask Him anything—anything! And yet He is not any kind of a vending machine for miracles, favors, and blessings. No, He is the friend who will do anything for me that is in His power to do because we have a relationship. We are intimate friends. I feel confident, even bold just to ask Him for favors for my friends or for people I see who need help I can't give. Knowing Him has opened my eyes to a lot of need. People need Him, and He knows it. I know it too.

Now I'm going to let you in on a secret hunch I have. I'm not sure this is in the Bible, but sometimes.....sometimes I think He answers my requests for help just because we share this closeness—you know, personally. I know it seems strange. Seems like He is playing favorites. So here's how I know this is true. Sometimes He will answer me by saying basically He's not going to do it—like it's not the right time or place or something. That's when I just smile at Him and stand my ground, making preparations here in faith, as if He's going to answer my request in the next five minutes.

And you know what? Yeah, He does it! Not like a machine or a robot, mind you. No, more like a friend who is worn down by my persistent insistence. That's when I know for sure that He and I have a really special relationship.

III

The Preacher

I am Miriam. If you had known me before I met the Lord, you would never in a million years have thought I would be a preacher. First of all, I came from a little backwater town that no one ever heard of. It was such an ordinary place, with ordinary people leading ordinary lives. I used to call it "Dullsville" –really!

Opportunities seemed limited there. Everyone around me had such fixed expectations for me. But I wanted more. I wanted to experiment, to see for myself whether something was good or bad. I went down a very dark path and got into a lot of trouble. What was worse, I found myself trapped in that lifestyle. Once I was in it, I couldn't get out.

I felt hopeless and depressed. Death looked like the only doorway out of this situation, but I couldn't quite bring myself to do it. One day in my weariness I sat down on a park bench to rest. An older woman, overweight and maybe in her 50s, sat down also. She looked around, cleared her throat, and began talking.

"I know why you're sitting here, dearie. You're looking for a way out." I stared at her. Who was this woman? How did she know anything about my situation?

"There's only one person who can get you out of this—and his name is Jesus."

Religion?! I didn't want to hear that. I started to rise from the bench. But she put her hand on my arm and said, "Wait! God sent me here today to speak to you," and she began telling me things about my life that no one knew. My mouth dropped open and I sat down again.

"Now don't you think that you should hear me out?" And she began to tell me about the salvation that was already available for me. "Yeah, yeah," I thought, "I've heard it before." But suddenly this was different. It was like I could see myself surrounded by darkness, but someone was approaching me with a lantern.

She continued, "Today would be a good day for you to start a new life, wouldn't it?" And she led me in a short prayer. I didn't feel much different as I prayed—except a big weight lifted off of me. I didn't know what it was at the time, but now I would say it was a big load of guilt and shame. The woman left me with a small gospel tract with the name of a church on the back. I found myself in the neighborhood of that church one morning and stopped in.

It's been years since I made that first step through the door of the Kingdom. Nowadays you might find me in almost any one of a dozen countries on the face of the earth. I've been to so many! Nevertheless, I'm not famous in the world, but I am known in Heaven. I just take what God gives me and spread it out before the people who come across my path. I've helped many churches get started, but my favorite encounter is meeting those who never darken the door of a church—the ones who feel trapped and in despair like I did.

I love to put them into His hand.

IV

The Disciple

I am Miriam. I remember the day I first knew Him, first knew His voice. It was not an audible voice. It was a voice so quiet that if I had not stilled my own voice within me, I would not have heard it. It was then I began to have confidence in the scripture that says, "My sheep hear My voice."

How did I get started on this practice of silence before Him? Let's see now. It was years ago. My own initial experience with the gift of salvation was so life-changing, that I wanted all that God had for me. I was hearing about people in my own time in history who were having wonderful encounters with God. They said they were "baptized in the Holy Spirit." So I pursued this experience also. And yes, when I finally had this experience, it did have some supernatural manifestations about it.

But the big thing for me was the Bible-reading. It totally changed for me—and that changed me. After my initial salvation experience, the Bible had come alive to me, as if I had never read it before. But after my experience with the Holy Spirit, it seemed as if Jesus Himself was sitting with me as my teacher when I read the Bible. I would read the words to myself, and then suddenly it was as if a voice inside me said, "What does <u>*that*</u> *mean?" or "What do you think about that?"*

Then gradually, as time went on, a picture would form inside me when I read Scripture. It would be a picture of Him sitting across the table from me, looking right at me. At first, I was afraid to look at Him too closely, and I felt shy. But eventually I saw that He was actually smiling at me. I began to see that His questions were friendly questions, meant for me to dig deeper and open myself up to the truth I was reading in His Word.

And then His interactions with me took on a different flavor. He began to talk to me as I was walking down the street or when I was eating alone at a restaurant, not just when I was reading my bible. I would hear His voice in my heart, and I knew it was Him because it was the same person as the one asking me those questions about my Scripture reading. I didn't feel His presence with me all the time, but I knew that He said in His Word that He would never leave us or forsake us. After a time, I just began to believe that whenever I turned to Him to ask Him a question, He would hear me.

And then I started noticing changes in me. I no longer wanted to do some things I used to like doing. Yeah, some of those things were sinful. But other things were not bad in themselves. It's just that more and more, I wanted to do things I knew would please Him—on purpose.

Some of my habits changed for sure. Certain things He actually spoke to me about. But He was so kind in His manner to me, I knew He spoke from love. I found out pretty quickly that anything He asked me to put aside or change for His sake, He would give me grace—supernatural help—to actually walk it out with Him.

You know, as of this day, I still have not seen Him with my natural eyes. And yes, I do know that the Bible says He is always with me, in some sense. But sometimes He is intensely with me. (I can feel His presence with me as I am speaking this.) I love these moments with Him!

I hear that He does give others even more direct experiences with Him, taking them into Heaven for visits and the like. I would love to have those experiences also. But in the meantime I will just keep looking at Him with my heart and listening to the words He gives me. And as I do so, I will grow more and more like Him—just like my Rabbi.

Which one of these four stories did you sense the greatest connection with? Or for which story would you say, "I would like to be like *that* woman"? Go back to that story and read it aloud again, but this time imagine that *you* are this Miriam—that you are describing *your* life. Before you begin, just say something like, "Holy Spirit, make this experience real for me." And if none of these four women prompt you to say, "I would like to be like *that* woman," take a few moments right now and write a few sentences about the ideal woman *you* would like to be.

Even in a male-dominant culture, the Miriams of Scripture had powerful ministries. Even when their culture relegated them to the back room or to a background role in the world, God did not. At key moments God put them in the spotlight, giving each of them a significant and key role in the history of faith recorded in Scripture. All of them lived either before the time of the Cross or just after, during a time of transition.

Let's take a moment and put some different labels on these portraits of Miriams. Here is what we have called them so far:

- the Watcher
- the Quick-witted Intercessor
- the Prophetess
- the Ark of the Presence
- the Faithful Mother and Wife
- the Meditative
- the Intimate Intercessor
- the Strong Presence at the Cross
- the Pentecostal Believer
- Set Free by the Messiah
- the Faithful Disciple of Messiah
- the Strong and Faithful Friend
- the Heart of a Servant
- the Preacher of the Good News
- the Contemplative Disciple
- the Extravagant Worshipper
- the Helper
- the Hard Worker
- the Mother of John Mark

If we named them according to their function in the Body of Christ, here is another way to label these portraits:

- Mystic
- Priest
- Prophet
- Temple of God
- Giver of Life
- Monk
- Priest
- Pillar
- Spirit-filled believer
- Delivered from darkness
- Disciple of Jesus
- Friend of God
- Obedient servant
- Evangelist
- Bride of Christ
- Worshipper
- Deacon
- Devoted servant
- Generous and hospitable giver

Some of those titles on the second list need no explanation, but others may not be so obvious. Let me elaborate a little. By "**Mystic**" I mean someone who likes to function somewhat or even a whole lot in the realm of the spirit, as opposed to focusing only on the natural realm that we can contact with our physical senses. A mystic might be someone who sees or perceives things with her spirit or heart. She might be someone who has what others would call "crazy supernatural adventures" with God or with His angelic beings.

A "**Priest**" is a go-between, from the heart of God to the people on earth. As such, the priest ministers to God, first and foremost. Out of that position and relationship of trust and intimacy, the priest brings people in her heart with her as she comes into the presence of God. Then after a time of connection with Him in that presence, the priest administrates the heart of God back to those people, releasing to them His desire for their lives. In Christ we are a "royal priesthood" (I Peter 2:9).

A "**Prophet**" is someone devoted to God, through whom God speaks and brings new revelation into the earth, through the prophet's interactions with the Lord and adventures in the unseen realms of the spirit.

A person who is a "**Temple of God**" is someone who carries the presence of God. The body of every believer in God is supposed to be a temple of the Holy Spirit, a place where God indwells (I Corinthians 6:19).

A "**Giver of Life**" in this context is a parent who not only brings the child into the world but also trains the soul of the child so that he or she is launched onto God's path in life.

A "**Monk**" is someone who gives his/her life over to meditating on God and the issues of life. Most particularly a person with the heart of a monk is a ponderer of the truths of God and their connection with life on earth.

A "**Pillar**" is someone who strengthens others by their example. The steadiness of the Pillar holds things together for others and with others in tough situations.

A "**Spirit-filled believer**" is one who is filled with the Holy Spirit—one who has been baptized, or immersed in the Holy Spirit, not once but over and over again, so that the believer is living a vibrant, active life in the realm of the spirit while still on the earth.

By "**Delivered from darkness**" I mean someone who, yes, may have literally had devils or demons cast out from them, but at a minimum has been freed from patterns or strongholds of destructive behavior, if not from the grasp of evil.

A "**Friend of God**" is someone who has an intimate relationship with Him. Jesus said to His disciples on the night He was betrayed, "***No longer do I call you slaves,*** *for the slave does not know what his master is doing;* ***but I have called you friends,*** *for all things that I have heard from My Father I have made known to you*" (John 15:15). [emphasis added in bold]

A "**Friend of God**" is someone to whom the Lord reveals Himself and the secrets or revelations of the Kingdom of Heaven.

A "**Bride of Christ**" is also an intimate friend of the Lord but in the context of a complete yielding, a **desire for oneness**, that leads that individual (male or female) to spend time contemplating His heart, gazing into His face in wordless prayer, with a life of oneness and union with the divine nature as the ultimate goal.

A "**Deacon**" in this context is a responsible, serving administrator. A deacon in Scripture was a person who "waited tables"—supervised the daily distribution of food to the poor. This is a person with a serving heart but also some ability to organize and inspire others to work together.

Now that you have a better idea of what I meant by those titles in the second list, take a closer look at the list. What title(s) attract you? Yes, I know all of them are good. But some or perhaps one of them draws your heart more than the rest.

If you really are having trouble with this exercise, take them two at a time. (You could even write them on small pieces of paper and draw them out of a pile two at a time.) Ask yourself: "Mystic? Or Priest?" Then take the "winner" from that pair and compare it to the next one on the list or the next one among the several you can't decide among. If the descriptive titles in the second list are off-putting or even offensive to you, take a breath and look at the first list again. Which of these attracts you?

Maybe you have a good idea about the purpose God has in mind for you, at least at this point in your life. And maybe that purpose is really not represented by any of the titles on these two lists. That's wonderful! You're ready to participate in the second phase of this exercise.

Second Phase

Now at this second phase, I would like you to do another holy experiment with me. If you narrowed down the titles in one of the lists to one title, OR if you already know what your purpose in this part of your life is about, you are ready for this experiment.

First, write a simple paragraph that describes you functioning as whatever attracted you or as what you believe your purpose is. Write down what you are doing, where you are doing it, and how it makes you feel to be functioning this way—or how you imagine it *would* feel if you ever got to do this.

Then I want you to read it aloud. Have you written this as if it is happening now? Or did you write it only as something maybe happening in the future? Let's rewrite it now (remember, it was only about one paragraph), and this time write it in the present, as if it's happening now. Instead of "I'd like to be the intimate friend of God," write "I am the intimate friend of God…." Then continue the rest of the paragraph in the same manner, writing as if it's happening now, as if you're living it now.

OK, now for the experiment. Have you ever read this verse in Job: "***You will also decree a thing***, *and it will be established for you; and light will shine on your ways*" (22:28)? Here's a similar one from the book of Proverbs: "***With the fruit of a man's mouth*** *his stomach will be satisfied; he will be satisfied with the product of his lips. Death and life are in* ***the power of the tongue***, *and those who love it will eat its fruit.*" (18:21-22)

Jesus said something similar that tracks with this: "*Truly I say to you, **whoever says to this mountain,** 'Be taken up and cast into the sea,' and does not doubt in his heart, but believes that what he says is going to happen, it will be granted him. Therefore I say to you, all things for which you pray and ask, **believe that you have received them, and they will be granted you***" (Mark 11:23-24) [emphasis added in bold]. He was teaching his disciples about how to activate faith: by speaking words connected with your heart, the place where your faith lives.

It's kind of like taking a rope and throwing it out in front of your path to "lasso" or catch on something in the future ahead of you, and then drawing it to yourself (or drawing *you* into your preferred future!)

Now take what you have written—that paragraph—and every day for the next 21 days I want you to read it aloud three times. It could be three times, one right after another, or it could be one reading three different times during the day. When you read it, put some passion behind it. (And if you can't do that, you probably are not so excited about becoming that person you wrote about.)

Now at the end of the 21 days, stop and assess. Did this make any difference at all? What kind of difference *should* this make? Well, it could be that during the 21 days you started noticing books, videos, sound files, conferences, classes, etc. that related to what you had written. Perhaps you noticed yourself actually being more aware of opportunities to function in that way, or you began to meet people who could help you develop in that direction. Maybe you even stepped out and acted on those opportunities.

So what's the point of all this?

ALL THE MIRIAMS OF SCRIPTURE WERE VERY HUMAN! All of them made big mistakes, like we do—things that show us they were far from perfect, that their lives could have ended in failure and bitterness...**BUT GOD HAD A DIFFERENT DESTINY FOR EACH OF THEM.** God also has a different destiny for YOU, my friend, a destiny beyond the mistakes and wrong turns your life has taken up to this point. He is calling all of His "Miriams," all of us ordinary women, for extraordinary exploits of ministry, to live the chronicles of the Kingdom of Heaven while we are still on the earth. Then what about you? You don't have to have the name Miriam to live your life like a Miriam in the Kingdom! Join me in prayer now—for ourselves and all the other "Miriams":

> *Father,*
>
> *Thank You that it is not too late for any of us to walk out our destiny in You.*
>
> *May the heart of every person who reads any portion of this book be drawn to pursue a greater vision for their own life.*
>
> *Most of all, may our eyes be open to hear Him who is calling us to see Him as He truly is....*

Made in the USA
Monee, IL
04 March 2024

54151589R00079